# When the Brook Dries Up

## Inspiration & Hope for Facing Life's Challenges

By Blondina Howes Jeffrey

*WHEN THE BROOK DRIES UP*
*Inspiration & Hope for Facing Life's Challenges*
By Blondina Howes Jeffrey

Copyright © 2012 Blondina Howes Jeffrey

Say So Books
Hollywood, FL
Library of Congress Control Number: 2012922860

ISBN 978-0-9885426-2-4

All Scripture references are taken from the Ryrie Study Bible King James Version, copyright © 1976, 1978 by The Moody Bible Institute Press, Chicago, USA.

*He Who Holds Us in His Hands*, words & music by Bryan Jeffery Leech © copyright 1988 Fred Bock Music Company. All rights reserved. Used by permission.

# Contents

# Dedication

To the memory of my parents William & Catherine Howes – whose lives mirrored to their children the meaning of faith, hope, and trust in the living God, and to the memory of the Pentecostal Church at Wapping, Montserrat, its walls now buried under volcanic mud and ash, where I was nourished and nurtured in the Christian faith.

And to all who shared your stories with me for this book.

# Acknowledgments

❧

Highest praise is due to Almighty God, my Heavenly Father, for His help in the publication of this second edition of *When the Brook Dries Up...Inspiration & Hope for Facing Life's Challenges*. He provided all I needed every step of the journey.

Special thanks to my dearest husband, Alfred, for your encouragement, helpful feedback and for always challenging me to be the best I could be. Thank you to all of you for your help in selling and circulating the first edition of my book: my siblings (Lazelle, Orwin, Oral, Easton); my sister-in-law, Karen; my niece Christine; my cousins Deborah, Beres and Ethlyn; and dear friends Pastor Ruth and Bernice (Rosanna Newton). Your unequivocal affirmation is sincerely appreciated. Without you, this second edition would not be a reality.

To my church family at the North Street Zion Church of God in Antigua, my sincere appreciation. Your support has been amazing. Special thanks to: Sharon Matthew and Aglow International, Antigua; Sharon and Del Looby Pilgrim.

To friends and churches in St. Maarten, the UK and USA – thanks to you, my brothers and sisters. Bishop Michael Greenaway, Pastors Ruthlyn Bradshaw, Martin Gerald, Roger Wade, Elvina Greenaway, Dr. George Irish – thank you! Doris Francis, Debbie Ryan, Viola Harley, Josepha Fenton, Joel Webbe, I appreciate your strong support.

I gratefully acknowledge those of you who shared your stories with me. *"The Lord God bringeth you into a good land, a land of brooks and water..." (Deuteronomy 8:7).*

Heartfelt thanks to Jim Kochenburger for your helpful interventions, your encouragement, and affirmation. Thanks for your support in the publication of this second edition of my book.

To God be all the glory!

# Introduction

*"...hope thou in God...*
*who is the health of my countenance, and my God."*
*Psalm 42:1b*

In the hit musical and motion picture, *Fiddler on the Roof*, Tevye, the indomitable leading character sang that at times life can leave us with our hearts lying "panting on the floor." Centuries before Tevye, another Jewish man, a patriarch named Job lamented the brevity and anguish of this experience called *"life"*:

> *"Man that is born of a woman is of few days, and full of trouble.*
> *He cometh forth like a flower, and is cut down: he fleeth also as a*
> *shadow and continueth not" (Job 14:1-2).*

*When the Brook Dries Up* is a book about life – its ups and downs, and joys and sorrows. It's about God's answers and His seeming silence. It's about relational disappointments, job losses, financial setbacks, ill health and other such things. But it is also about the answer to these baffling, puzzling issues.

These experiences which I have mentioned are ubiquitous. These days especially, a person does not have to go far to find someone who has been hurt or disappointed by life. Just last night, one of my siblings shared with me the various health issues he is facing. "When it is not one thing, it is the next," he concluded. That's true. This is *life*!

A few months ago, another young man shared with me some devastating news he had just received. He said that many nights he wished he did not have to wake up the next morning. His question to God was, "Why me?" This is *Life…*

The problem of pain and trouble is fundamental to life and has been dealt with by myriad books and writers. However, a dichotomy remains, particularly for the Christian. It lies in the fact that the gospel we preach teaches about a God who is good, just, righteous, and all-powerful, who truly "has the whole world in His hands." If this is so, then the question is always with us about the "whys" of sufferings and tragedies, especially when they happen to "good" and "undeserving" people, to innocent children, or to beloved children of God who spend their entire lives serving and following this God.

The problem for many has deepened in our twenty-first century, because more than ever before, "blessings" of material prosperity, health, healing (and the like) are touted as the inalienable right and entitlement of the Christian. The promulgation of televangelism has made the experience of those who are struggling, for whom life seems just not to be working, even harder to bear – especially as they hear others testify to "proving God" because they gave more or did more, and as a result, saw all their problems solved and difficulties go away.

To be fair to those who think that wealth and health are the entitlement of the believer, they are able to quote many scriptures from the Bible that seem to infer that pain, suffering, and trouble do not belong to the child of God, but to the ungodly. Indeed, they argue, it is God's desire and determination that *"(we) prosper and be in health, even as (our) soul prospers" (3 John 2)*.

Deuteronomy 27 is one of the scriptures quoted to support this point of view. There, Moses catalogs and lists the blessings which will overtake the Israelites if they are obedient to God's laws and commands, as opposed to the curses and woes which would accompany their disobedience. The obvious inference here is that material and other physical blessings are a sign of God's favor, whereas sickness, disease, want, and material poverty characterize His displeasure. These are thoughts which shape the belief system, thinking, and teaching of many televangelists in our day!

Yet, the reality for many a child of God is the opposite. Many suffer debilitating ill health. Many barely eke out a living. Many have seen marriages and close relationships fall apart. Many have children who don't turn out the way they expected, and many find their plans and dreams unfulfilled.

So how then do we address the ambivalence of believers who are not among the "blessed" lot of those who have prospered and lived in health, even as their soul prospered? Is it because their soul is not prospering? Is it because their faith is so little and weak? Is it because they are in disobedience to the commands and will of God? Or are God's "blessings" (so-called) only for the select few?

The reality is, for as many Christians as experience the blessings of health, wealth, and prosperity, there are countless others who suffer prolonged hardship in their Christian walk with God. They see no light at the end of their tunnel, and they have become wary and tired of religious talk and platitudes. In fact, their brooks have dried up.

One of the ways many deal with this issue is to become introspective and, consequently, discouraged. Believers can begin to compare themselves with others or become overly hard on themselves, continually and obsessively returning to some "wrong" they might have committed and wallowing in guilt over it, when in fact, God has forgiven them long ago. They do this in an effort to identify their sin, their problem – the reason why God seems to be angry with them.

The irony of the matter is that it is not only people who suffer financially and physically that sit beside dried-up brooks. There are many who have reached the pinnacle of their dreams and have experienced great success in life – wealth, popularity, fame – yet they sit every day beside a dried-up brook. If they were to be honest, they would tell you that deep inside, there is emptiness and dryness, with each day of their lives as joyless as the other. They are wealthy and healthy, but they are in a hard place...where no water is. Their brooks of contentment, joy, hope and peace have dried up!

So, bewildered Christian, do you really think the answer is in getting a job (or a better job), in material wealth, or in overcoming your health issues? I am not promoting poverty and ill health, neither condemning wealth nor good health. There is nothing wrong with being healthy and wealthy. In fact, the Bible states in Ecclesiastes 10:19 that money answers all things. In Proverbs 22:7, the Bible says that the borrower is servant to the lender. But nowhere in the Scriptures is the believer promised that on this journey beneath the sun, on his way from earth to Heaven, he is entitled to material wealth, health, the good life, or that these are evidences of God's good favor – nor that all we need to do is "name it and claim it."

In Psalm 73, Asaph is baffled by the seeming prosperity and trouble-free life of the ungodly in contrast to the struggles that seemed to overwhelm him. He almost slipped into the heretical belief that he was wasting his time serving God. But he realized his error. He came to understand that the issue was not about health and wealth and the problem-free life, but it was about God. Job too, after having argued his deservedness, was blessed with a revelation of God's character and learned that God's blessings were in no way tied to his material or physical state. God's blessings were bound up in His character and in knowing and understanding who God is. He finally acknowledges God's wisdom and infinite divine purpose, and lays his hands on his mouth: *"I abhor myself and repent in dust and ashes" (Job 42:6).*

*When the Brook Dries Up* offers no easy platitudes. It invites you on a journey to a place called Zarephath. On this journey you will meet a prophet, a widow woman, a bewildered dad, a divorcee, a dejected executive, and a woman whose dreams were interrupted by debilitating illness and disease, among others. These folks are not fairy tale characters. They are ordinary people like you and me, who have sat and watched their brooks dry up *only to find that dried-up brooks can be the onset for the miraculous.*

So, if you feel discouraged and disappointed with God, you will find encouragement here. If you are baffled about life, with its unexpected turns and interruptions, you will be introduced to the answer here. If you have it all – money, fame, wealth, and health, but in spite of the glitter and glitz, you feel jaded with life, you will find inspiration and purpose here. If you have been helplessly staring at your dried-up brook, you will find hope here.

*When the Brook Dries Up* is not a secret about optimistic and positive thinking – as useful as some have posited that to be. Neither is it about finding your inner strength, because for many, that too has dried up. It finds the answer in an eternal, true, and living God who reveals Himself to those who seek Him and even to those who do not.

This second edition of *When the Brook Dries Up*, just like the first, reaffirms the eternal character of a just, righteous, good, and sovereign God. It reminds us that this God never forgets His children, never forsakes them, and will never let go of their hands even in their most troubling experiences.

As you read, you will see that this God is true, faithful, and trustworthy. In any and every situation, He works all things for His own glory and for our best good.

# Preface

He moved to the United States from a small Caribbean island. He wanted to make life better for himself and his family. He was sure he would. It took him some time before he was able to find a job, but eventually, with his MBA degree, he secured quite a good one in an upper middle class area in New England. It was beautiful there, very much like the Caribbean island he had just left.

He worked hard and got a few promotions, but he always felt that he was being kept one step behind. He did not feel satisfied with his job and wanted to provide so much more for his family. He felt he needed much more money than what he was making if he were to give his children the type of life he felt they deserved.

In the meantime, some incomprehensible things began to take place in his life. First of all, his dreams for a son came true on his birthday, April 21, 1986. He'd had two beautiful daughters, and seven years had passed since his last daughter was born. He and his wife did not expect any more children, but then a beautiful son arrived. Trouble set in almost immediately. Without any warning and with the doctors unable to understand why, all the organs in the little baby's body began to shut down. The man was devastated.

His anguish and anxiety were almost unbearable. Unable to sleep at night, he tells of how he and his two young daughters drove around the city in their car, praying and crying, and playing the song "Somebody Somewhere Is Praying for You," over and over again. That song somehow gave them a sense of peace, and solace, and hope. He had called his sisters and father still living in the Caribbean. He knew they were praying. And there were others too: his in-laws in the US, his other siblings in the UK, and his church family.

Miraculously, the baby recovered. The doctors could not explain how or why. The man knew how and why. It was a miracle.

But there was more to follow that year. One afternoon, as he waited to take the train to a work appointment, a crazed man he had never seen before and who did not know him, pushed him onto the tracks as a train was approaching.

He looked death in the face, but in those few seconds of panic and indescribable fear, he made a decision which perhaps saved his life. "I knew I was going to die," he said, "so with all the strength I had in me, I threw myself onto the train rather than allow myself to fall onto the tracks." Tons of steel colliding with flesh flung his body back onto the platform area. Horrified, several people rushed to his aid, certain that he was dead. Others caught and detained his attacker. The medics were summoned and he survived. It was another miracle.

His recovery was long and slow. It ate up all his savings. He was advised to hire an attorney for compensation, and the directors at his workplace suggested a law firm that was supposed to be good. His lawyer constantly assured him that he was moving on with the case, but never did anything. The deadline for the statute of limitations passed. He found out later that the law firm was on retainer to the Transit Board which owned the trains and subway system. He had been living in the United States for only two years by that time. He did not know who to turn to and the case died. The criminal case against his attacker was dismissed. The verdict was "not guilty by reason of insanity."

He was determined to get on with his life. He struggled after this to make ends meet and he was able to, especially with the help of his father and siblings.

Then a new company opened up that appeared to be the gateway to the life he wanted. He was lured away from his old job by the offer of a 30% salary increase. He prayed for God to close the door if it was not His will, so when it remained open he felt quite certain that God had opened the door for him. He went through it gladly.

Then the bubble burst. Just a year and a half after he moved to the new job, the bosses at work walked in and declared that they were closing the operation; that day was the last day of work for everyone. He was terrified. This could not be happening. He had just turned 50.

Seven years have passed since then, and his life has been one of trying one thing and the next without success. He has faced many closed doors. Not much has worked for him, he feels.

At times he barely manages to keep a roof over his family's heads and food on the table. He knows that it is nothing short of a miracle that he is able to do this. His situation has been protracted and humbling... no, humiliating. After all, he has an MBA. He has no idea what the future holds for him. His financial brook dried up long ago.

Many times he has felt like giving up – really throwing in the towel. He felt like forgetting about God and everything else. Barely eking out a living every day of his life. Barely making it. Nothing in his horizon suggests rain. His brook of faith has slowed many times to just a trickle... almost dried up.

And he has prayed and believed and given and paid his tithes and fasted and served God *"with the multitude who keep the holy day" (Psalm 42:4)*. But no cloud the size of a man's hand has appeared in the sky. If it has, it always turned out to be a mirage, illusory, leaving him feeling worse than before. There is no sound of the abundance of rain. His brook has dried up.

He listens to all the prosperity apologists, the "name it and claim it" contenders, and he wonders why it is so different with him. Why is his life one empty promise after another?

And he knows what it means to feel fear. This dried-up brook experience has been frightening. But he keeps it mostly to himself, sometimes letting out bits of it to his siblings. Sometimes. But he has very often felt worn down. Tired and afraid of today and even more so of tomorrow. At times it is as if he cannot take one more step. Parched and dry. Discouraged and despondent. Dried up...

Though he does not know what the future holds and though he has often wanted to give up and disappear from this reality, he has somehow found that every single difficult, anxious morning he has been given the strength to keep going, to keep trying – in the face of insurmountable odds.

He thinks all his brooks have dried up – but...

# Chapter 1

## Brooks That Go Dry

⟨ornament⟩

*"And it came to pass after a while, that the brook dried up..."*
*1 Kings 17:7*

The idea for this book was born partly out of a discussion my husband and I had one morning about the idea of God being "more than enough." We mulled over this thought particularly with regards to overwhelming situations some people have to face in life.

We discussed the question, how is it true that God is more than enough? In really practical terms, how is this lived out on a day-to-day basis? We were plunged into an ocean of questioning and soul searching.

How, in all practicality, we pondered, is God more than enough when debilitating illness strikes? When close and once cherished relationships break up and there are no pieces left to pick up? When job loss makes the threat of homelessness imminent? When creditors pursue you mercilessly? When you watch helplessly as all the things that gave you stability, independence, and control slip hopelessly out of your grip?

And it is not that you have not prayed. You have, with fasting and firm belief, countless times. You have hoped for a breakthrough – for some sign of relief, but instead, you are met with deafening silence.

Have you ever been there?

The narrative in 1 Kings 17:1-16 unfolds during the reign of King Ahab. Ahab was one of the most ungodly and wicked kings the land of Israel had ever seen. He began ruling after his father Omri died. Omri himself was an evil king who had caused the people of Israel to sin against the God of Israel through idol worship.

Following in his father's footsteps, Ahab married Jezebel, a cruel and domineering pagan woman, the daughter of a king of the Zidonians. At the time of the narrative, Ahab had built an altar for Baal in the house of Baal, and he himself had become an idol worshipper, along with many of the people of Israel.

It is at this point in the history of God's people, the Israelites, that Elijah the Tishbite emerges. He appears on the scene as if out of nowhere and prophesies that the land and people of Israel will experience a terrible drought. Implicit in his pronouncement is the idea of God's direct intervention and punishment. *"As the Lord God of Israel liveth before whom I stand..." (1 Kings 17:1).* The prophet is speaking on behalf of the Lord God of Israel, as His servant and as His prophet. He confidently avows that rain will not fall again *"but according to my word" (1 Kings 17:1).* His word and God's are one. He is the prophet of God.

Just as he predicted, the rains stop, and for three and a half years no rain falls, and neither is there dew on the ground. The narrative does not detail the effect of the drought on the people of the land. That is left to the readers' imagination. The widow woman's situation highlighted in this account gives us a microscopic view of what countless others must have experienced.

The story in 1 Kings 17 really focuses on Elijah and God's sustenance of His prophet and the widow woman. Once his pronouncement is given, Elijah is instructed to go to the brook Cherith where God tells him he would drink from the brook and be fed by ravens. Without fail, morning and evening, ravens arrive with meat and bread, and Elijah drinks from the brook and is sustained.

After a while, as is to be expected, the brook dries up. The Scripture omits any reference to Elijah's reaction to this development. Neither are we told how soon after this he is instructed to go to Zarephath, where a widow woman had already been prepared by God to feed him.

At Zarephath, at the gate of the city, Elijah encounters a woman who turns out to be the widow woman of whom God had spoken. He asks her for some water and then for a piece of bread. In spite of her destitution, she makes a meal for Elijah before making one for herself and her son, only to then discover a miracle! She, her son, and Elijah are sustained throughout the remainder of the drought.

This account lays the foundation for this book.

Strained relationships. Financial distress. Physical, emotional, and mental anguish. All of these are very often the bedfellows of dried-up brooks. *But dried-up brooks can also mark the onset of the miraculous.*

The following chapters will look at the difficulties we can face, but also God's efficacy at the times of "dried-up brooks." Perhaps your dried-up brook was once a gushing river of health, or financial independence and stability, or a rippling stream of love flowing between you and a spouse or dear friend. Or maybe it was the youthful zest of hopes, dreams, aspirations, and possibilities, or the comfort of social usefulness and prominence.

You have had to sit by your brook and watch it dry up. And as yet, you have not seen your Zarapheth!

Can God be trusted at such times? Do we ever get "more than we can bear"? Is this God of the Bible truly enough or even "more than enough" in such times?

Is it really true that when we come to the end of all we have and have held dear, and are left only with God, we will find that He is more than enough?

If it is really true, *how is it true?* For the person whose dreams are shattered, who is facing prolonged adversity, indomitable challenges, insurmountable odds, open doors that lead to nowhere, and hopes that seem to dim with each passing year – *How is this true?*

Have you ever felt as if your brook of faith was drying up? Have you struggled with your faith in God and His goodness, or with your faith not so much in His *ability*, but in His *willingness* to come to your help? Have you ever felt that He just seems not to care?

Have you ever been there?

Have you ever felt disappointed, let down by God – afraid that your beliefs and all you were taught from childhood may not be true? Have you ever feared that they may all be a fantasy? Have you ever wondered if it is all nothing more than a desperate, nostalgic attempt to hold on to childhood and childish beliefs once held dear – an attempt to preserve some spiritual heritage passed on by parents and significant others in your life?

Have you ever been there?

Have you ever felt misled? Mistaken? So sure of God's leading, only to find that you are hurtling headlong down into an abyss of fear, guilt, doubt, discouragement, unanswered prayers, and unfulfilled dreams?

Have you ever been there?

Have you ever wondered what you did wrong? Have you ever agonized that you must be displeasing God in some way, and returned countless times to some past wrong, rehearsing it in your mind, over and over again, thinking that this struggle you are going through must be your punishment?

Have you ever pondered how life seems to work for others – but not for you? That health and wealth just evades you? That the "name it and claim it" promise remains just beyond your reach?

*Have you been there? I mean – at a dried-up brook?*

This book is not an apology for religion. It is not a treatise, nor a how-to book. It will not give you seven steps to discovering the "more than enough" God, or how to get out of the "dried -up brook" syndrome. But it will attempt, through an exploration of the account in 1 Kings 17, to look at the experience of "dried-up brooks" in relation to the provision of God.

Elijah obeyed God explicitly. He did exactly what he was directed to do, yet his brook dried up. When so many other prophets in Israel bowed their knees to Baal, Elijah remained faithful to Jehovah – even with threats against his life.

*But Elijah was there – at a dried-up brook – and we do not know for how long.*

But this book is not just about the experience of Elijah the Tishbite. The story of the man in the opening pages is true. And just as true are the testimonies shared in this book of others who have also faced dried-up brooks. This book has been inspired by their lives, ordinary people like you and me, believers, dear children of God, and followers of the Lord Jesus Christ who have tried to faithfully follow the Lord and devoted their lives to Him in service. They have done all they could to be loyal and obedient, yet have sat by and watched helplessly as their brook slowed to a trickle and with rising panic, have seen it eventually dry up.

How do we find God to be more than enough in such times?

# Chapter 2

## Drought!

"As the Lord God of Israel liveth...there shall not be dew nor
rain these three years, but according to my word."
1 Kings 17:1

The worst drought in modern times occurred in Ethiopia in 1984-1985 with catastrophic results. An estimated 800,000 people perished! [1] This is unbelievably difficult to imagine. But that's what can happen when rain does not fall for a very long time.

The economic, environmental, and social impact of drought is typically grave. Everyone is affected and not only those who live in agrarian communities. Death, disease, inflation, unemployment, and many other social, economic, physical, and psychological woes can result.

The bottom line is that rain is essential to our survival.

We know that without water we would not stay alive. We need it to stay healthy. We need it for irrigation, industry, and growing food. We need it to drink, to bathe, and to keep ourselves and our surroundings clean. Human beings can live without food for several weeks, but survive only a few days without water. Next to the air that we breathe, water is our most important need.

Additionally, water makes up about 70% of our bodies. It's in our cells and in our blood. It controls our body temperature, helps us digest food, transports body waste, takes in oxygen, and lubricates our joints. Without rain we have no water. You see the cycle.

According to 1 Kings 17, no rain fell for not just one or two years, but three and a half! We can safely conclude that this drought posed monumental problems for the inhabitants of the land. Theirs was an agrarian society and economy. We don't have to wonder about the socioeconomic impacts. We know that as the brooks and rivers dried up, crops failed and people and animals perished. The suffering must have been horrendous. Death and suffering must have been everywhere, from the king's palace to the humblest of the homes in the land!

Even with no details given about its impact, through our mind's eye we can visualize what the drought looked and felt like. This poetic masterpiece in Jeremiah 14:1-6 describing a later severe drought in Jerusalem helps us:

*Judah mourneth, and the gates thereof languish; they are black to the ground; and the cry of Jerusalem is gone up.*

*And their nobles have sent their little ones to the waters: they came to the pits, and found no water; they returned with their vessels empty; they were ashamed and confounded, and covered their heads.*

*Because the ground is chapt for there was no rain in the earth, for the plowmen were ashamed, they covered their heads.*

*Yea, the hind also calved in the field, and forsook it, because there was no grass. And the wild asses did stand in the high places, they snuffed up the wind like dragons; their eyes did fail, because there was no grass.*

The suffering in Israel during those three and a half years was ubiquitous, severe, and protracted.

According to the scriptural account, this drought was actually brought on as a result of the prayer of God's prophet, Elijah. The people of Israel had turned to Baal worship, led by their evil king Ahab and his wicked wife,

Jezebel. They began to believe as the pagans did, that Baal controlled the rain. Elijah prayed for God to intervene by not allowing it to rain so that the people of Israel could see that the weather was not controlled by their so-called god, Baal, but by the Lord God of Israel.

The drought was punishment for their disobedience, waywardness, rebellion, and idolatry – as was the drought in Jeremiah's day. At the same time, it was intended to lead them back from idolatry to worship of the one true God, Jehovah. God, at the word of Elijah, withheld the rains for three and a half long years. From the king in his throne to the lowliest peasant in the field, everyone suffered the consequences.

*"The heavens became brass and the land iron" (Deuteronomy 28:30).*

## GOD AND NATURE

This account in 1 Kings 17, the account of the flood in Genesis chapters 6 – 8, the plagues that were rained on Pharaoh and the Egyptians in Genesis 8 – 10, and the parting of the Red Sea in Genesis 14, are some of the incontrovertible evidence in the Bible that God, Jehovah, is in control of nature and can use nature however He wishes – to punish, chasten, convince, convict, and protect.

Our concern here, however, is not God's role in natural disasters or His power over nature. The question at issue is, does God allow difficulties, dry times, and drought in the lives of His people? Does He send these times into our lives?

If we are to read the entire account, including James 5:17-18, we realize that God and Elijah worked in tandem. It was the prophet Elijah who prayed and asked God to shut up the heavens so that it would not rain. He yearned for his fellow Israelites. He was "jealous" for the Lord God of Israel. He wanted the people of Israel to choose to serve God and Him alone. He wanted them to forsake the worship of Baal and return to worshiping Jehovah – the God who had brought them out of Egypt. So he prayed earnestly that it would not rain, and it did not rain for three and a half years.

God is sovereign, but in ways that we find unexplainable, God allows man to be a part of His sovereign plan and power through prayer. God was working out His sovereign purpose in all of this, but it was Elijah's prayer that ushered in the years of drought. *The drought was sent so that the people of God could turn their backs on Baal worship and turn again to worship the true God.*

So, does God send drought and does He allow drought? Our conclusion is:

- God sends and allows drought or dry times in the lives of His people as a form of chastening for wrongdoing, disobedience, and rebellion.
- God sends and allows dry times for the express purpose of turning His people's hearts back to Him.
- Dry times happen because we are being tried, tested, and refined, and we will come forth as pure gold. After you have suffered a while, [God] will make you perfect, establish, strengthen, and settle you (1 Peter 5:10).
- Dry times happen because we live in a cursed world and therefore, sometimes, not for any specific reason.

## SPIRITUAL DRY TIMES AND THE CHURCH

We all experience spiritual dry times when it seems as if God has turned His back on a church, a nation, a people, a family, or a person.

In the case of a church, believers may become complacent, cold, and indifferent – just like the church in Laodicea. Many years may go by without any visible church growth. In fact, numbers may dwindle and the pastor may come to a place where he is only going through the motions. If it were left up to him, he would give up and walk away. But he stays on, simply because he is not one to give up. He has tried everything there is to try – but nothing seems to work. Many pastors are there.

Conversely, the church might be bursting at its seams with many people joining its membership, but righteous living, godliness, prayer, and the study of and obedience to God's Word may not be the hallmark of the lives of many of these church members.

Believers labor in the flesh. From the pulpit to the pew there is a lot of emotionalism and exuberance, but it is really all about us and not about God. But *"they that are in the flesh cannot please God" (Romans 8:8),* so God no longer honors the celebration and worship.

If the truth be told, many have grown so familiar with God that they have lost their fear and awe of Him. Were the Alpha and Omega (God) to write to the angel of this church, He would pronounce the same words He spoke to the church of Sardis in Revelation 3:1, *"I know thy works, that thou hast a name that thou livest and art dead."* These believers have entered into a dry place. Many, many churches are there.

## SPIRITUAL DRY TIMES AND THE BELIEVER

This is when the Christian feels distant and far away from his God. There is really no spiritual connection – not even when he tries to pray and read the Bible. In fact, the desire for those activities dissipates. He is assailed by doubts, though he continues to do the things he always did – attend church, witness, involve himself in all the activities and sacraments of the church. But in his heart he experiences dryness – no rain! No moisture in his life. He feels dead. He longs for the days when he felt God near.

*"My flesh longs for you in a dry and thirsty land, where no water is..." (Psalm 63:1).*

In Psalm 42 the psalmist, David, experienced some of this. It was a time when he wandered in the wilderness of Judah, running for his life from his archenemy, King Saul. He drew a parallel between his actual physical experience and what he had begun to experience spiritually. Having had to roam in the wilderness would have affected his times of worship, of meeting with God by himself and spending time with Him alone, and also meeting with his fellow worshippers who worshipped in the sanctuary. His circumstances were not of his own making. He had to run because of the Saul's threat on his life. But just as the wilderness was dry and barren, he found himself wandering spiritually in a drought-ridden place with no water.

He yearned for God as a hart *"panting after the water brooks" (Psalm 42:1).* So deep was his distress and longing for a different experience, a renewed life – a life filled with hope in God, that he found himself crying day and night because of his situation.

*"My tears have been my meat day and night..." (Psalm 42:3).*

He was so far away from God and His bountiful blessings that those around him began to question his validity as a believer. They figured that something was wrong. When you live for God, when you are His child, He always comes through for you.

*"Where is thy God?" (Psalm 42:3,10)*

He used to be a consistent churchgoer and worshipper. He had gone with the multitude to the house of God with the voice of joy and praise and he had kept the holy day – the Sabbath – as all were commanded to do. He had done all the right things, yet he was living in a dry place. He was experiencing drought.

It made him feel that his God had forgotten him – indeed forsaken him – and it made others pass judgment on him.

*"Where is thy God?"*

This dry experience made him feel dejected, despondent, cast down in spirit, and rejected by the very God he was trying to worship.

How do you respond to those who question your validity as a Christian? How do you respond when all the evidence seems to indicate that something is wrong with you, that indeed you are being punished? Nobody suffers such dry times in their lives, your questioners surmise, unless their God has forsaken them. And God will only forsake you when you have done things so terrible against Him that He has to step in and punish you.

That's what the psalmist's contemporaries thought, as many may do today:

*"Where is your God?"*

It was the question that haunted Job's wife as she suffered the loss of her possessions and her children and **witnessed** the sufferings of her husband. She entered into a dry wilderness, a spiritually dry wilderness. Her faith and trust in God simply evaporated.

*"Where is your God? If He is there, He is not of any benefit to you....
Curse Him and die..." (Job 2:9).*

These are the words of a woman who had witnessed firsthand the integrity of her husband, seen his steadfastness and faithfulness to God, and as long as she could remember could not recall that he ever turned aside from his worship of God and his trust in Him. All his losses were also her losses, children – all of them at one fell swoop – possessions, and finally his health. She reached her dry place. This was her place where there was no water. As far as she was concerned it was hopeless. In her wilderness of suffering she lost touch with God. Doubt and disappointment invaded her life and she jumped to sinful, irreverent, and heretical conclusions about God.

*"Where is your God? Curse Him and die."*

She had become spiritually dry.

Most of us have come down hard on Job's wife. But have we ever been there – in a dry place spiritually, where there is no water? She was totally and completely spiritually dry. She had nothing left in her. She felt no connection to God and in fact could have been very angry with Him.

## CAUSES OF SPIRITUAL DROUGHT

We have suggested that dry times happen in the lives of believers because God allows or sends these periods of drought, or because we live in a fallen world where such times occur for no particular reason. But what can be the specific causes of spiritual drought in a church or in our personal lives as believers?

- We fall away from God, leaving our first love (Revelation 2:10). The subtle offerings of the world tug at our heart strings and we fall prey to their allure and appeal. Our zeal and devotion to God wanes. We love God, but He is no longer first in our hearts and lives. The cares of this world and the deceitfulness of riches choke out God's Word, and we enter into a dry place.
- The insidiousness of self-reliance makes us believe that our knowledge, skills, and our talents and abilities are adequate. We know what we want and we know how to get what we want. We become idol worshippers. Smug and self-satisfied, we rely less on God and more on ourselves for the answers.
- We disobey, we rebel, we sin against God, grieving and quenching the Holy Spirit, and we enter into a dry place.
- Life experiences which are so calamitous and prolonged erode our hope, trust, and confidence in God. Our experiences draw us away from God instead of towards Him. Our strength is no longer being renewed because we are no longer waiting upon Him. The point to the parable of the unjust judge in Luke 18:1-8 is arresting. It is found

in verse 8: *"Nevertheless when the Son of Man cometh, shall he find faith on the earth?"* The believers' hope and trust in God can dry up!

- God is testing us. He has big plans for us and is taking us through the fire to burn out the dross. First Peter 5:10 says, *"But the God of all grace who hath called us to his eternal glory by Jesus Christ, after that ye have suffered a while, make you perfect, establish, strengthen, settle you."* There is the sound of abundance in rain.

## THE BELIEVER'S ASSURANCE

Spiritual drought and dry times in the life of the believer do not negate or invalidate the believer's position of security in God through Jesus Christ. The New Testament is replete with scriptures affirming the believer's security. Ephesians 1:4 tells us that the believer was chosen in Christ before the foundation of the world. John 10:25 declares that all believers are given to Jesus Christ by His Father and no one can pluck them out of His Father's hand. Finally, in Colossians 3:3 we read, *"For ye are dead, and your life is hid with Christ in God."*

The believer is secure because he is chosen.

The believer is secure because he is in the Father's hand.

The believer is secure because he is hidden with Christ in God.

This is the position of the believer – all believers. The challenge is not our position, but the daily working out of our salvation with fear and trembling. God has never been in the business of making robots. We are secure in Him, but day by day we face life, the world, the flesh, and the devil. We make decisions. "Prone to wander Lord I feel it, prone to leave the God I love…" [2] We sometimes wander away from God, lust after sinful things, and make a mess of our lives. Believers do. We live in a world which is not a friend to grace – which we so often seem to forget! And we succumb to the things around us and enter into dry places.

Dry times happen because we live in a world of ups and downs – good times and bad. Brooks dry up. Comforts we thought were bestowed by God fly away.

The believer's challenge is his response to the dried-up brook, to the prolonged drought in his life – failing health, diminished finances, prolonged unemployment, shattered hopes and dreams. What do we do when dry times come? To whom do we go for the answer?

Do we give up hope like Job's wife? Do we turn away from God in anger and despair? Do we get bitter and negative? Do we run and hide, fold our hands, throw in the towel, give up, and walk away?

Where do we really find the answer when we are at our lowest ebb?

# Chapter 3

## Cherith

*"Get thee hence...and hide thyself*
*by the brook Cherith, that is before Jordan."*
*1 Kings 17:3*

Cherith is a place God had prepared for His servant during the time of drought in Israel. It was a place of protection, rest, solitude, promise, and provision. But was Cherith a cruel joke? God promised Elijah He would provide for him there while the drought continued in the land of Israel. But the brook dried up...

### CHERITH – PLACE OF PROTECTION

*"Get thee hence, and turn thee eastward, and hide thyself by the brook Cherith" (1 Kings 17:3).*

My father often told us the story of a preacher who received a call one night to go pray for someone in a nearby village who was very ill. He immediately left on horseback to visit the sick person only to find on arrival at the home that the place was well lit, and that in fact there seemed to be a party going on. He knocked at the door and explained his mission, only to be told that no one at the house was ill, neither had they sent for him.

Somewhat perturbed and totally bewildered, he made his way back home, told his wife what had transpired, and eventually put the incident behind him.

Some years later, on one of his weekly visits to the local prison he was told that one of the prisoners wanted to speak with him. The man spoke to him as if he knew him, though the minister could not recall having met him before. The prisoner reminded him of the incident years before when he was called to visit a sick man in another village. The minister recalled the incident. The prisoner informed the minister that it had all been a sinister plot. He had been hired to kill the minister and was supposed to carry out the dastardly deed on the way to the village. He had followed the minister all the way to the village and back to his home, but was unable to accomplish his heinous mission because there were two other men traveling with the minister on horseback on either side of him, both on the way to the village and back to his home.

This time the minister was in complete shock. He assured the prisoner that he was alone that night. He remembered the night distinctly and informed him that there were no other people with him. The prisoner insisted that it was not so and insisted that the minister had been flanked by two men on horseback all the way to the village and all the way back home. Because of this the would-be assassin had been forced to discard his plans to kill him.

Awestruck, the minister realized that he had been protected that night by the angels of God.

That story had a great impact on me as a little girl and right into my adult years. It taught me emphatically that God protects His children in the face of dangers seen and unseen, and that the angels of the Lord do encamp around and deliver those who fear God (Psalm 34:7).

By predicting drought in Israel, Elijah was confronting and putting himself in conflict with the most fearsome of people in the land – Jezebel, Ahab's wife. She was a formidable foe, ruthless and domineering, a pagan woman who had slain hundreds of the prophets of Jehovah.

We also learn from Obadiah, Ahab's servant that Ahab had been searching for Elijah relentlessly. *"There is no nation or kingdom, whither my Lord hath not sent to seek thee..." (1 Kings 18:10).* So determined was Ahab to find Elijah that any nation or kingdom that said Elijah could not be found there had to swear by an oath that they spoke the truth. Later events showed that Jezebel did not hesitate to eliminate anyone who dared to defy or oppose her husband.

But God prepared a place of protection for His prophet. He sent him to the secluded brook Cherith. *"Get thee hence… and hide thyself"* (*1 Kings 17:3*).

God's protection of His children can be demonstrated in various ways and methods. This account in 1 Kings 17 includes three I will mention here:

- He may provide supernatural protection.
- He may use perfectly natural methods.
- We may be asked to use our common sense and run…

In 2 Kings 6, the king of Syria sent horses and chariots to Dothan to capture Elisha. Elisha and his servant awoke the following morning to see that a host of this king's army had surrounded them. But the Lord of Hosts sent His own army of protection. When the servant's eyes were "opened" he saw that the mountain was full of horses and chariots of fire surrounded Elisha.

Daniel, plotted against by presidents and princes because of envy and jealousy, was thrown into a den of lions. When King Darius realized how he had been duped and manipulated into being a part of orchestrating Daniel's demise, assured Daniel: *"Thy God whom thou servest continually, he will deliver you"* (*Daniel 6:16*). And did God deliver Daniel? God protected him all night right in the den of hungry lions. He tells the king the following morning: *"My God hath sent his angel, and hath shut the lions' mouths, that they have not hurt me"* (*Daniel 6:23*).

In the account in Acts 12, Peter was arrested by Herod and imprisoned, left to await his fate which would come after Easter. While he slept in prison, bound with chains between two soldiers, an angel came into the prison and engineered the most miraculous and daring escape – one worthy of a Hollywood script.

These three accounts are nothing short of supernatural!

Yet, when Herod intended to search out and kill the baby Jesus, God told Joseph in a dream to flee into Egypt for safety (Matthew 2:13-15). King David had to use his common sense and run from his beloved son Absalom, just as he did from King Saul. God can supernaturally protect or we may just have to use plain common sense and run away from clear and impending danger.

Elijah was in danger from Ahab and Jezebel. God commanded the prophet to hide himself. No heroics were required. You are in danger – hide. We might sometimes be tempted to think that as Christians we should never run, never hide because God should always miraculously protect us from danger. He does on occasion, but if we are in a position to do something to protect ourselves from impending danger, it might be folly to wait around expecting miraculous deliverance. We may be required to run away from the danger. We need to have the wisdom of God which makes us as wise as serpents yet harmless as doves (Matthew 10:16). It certainly does not show a lack of courage to get out of danger's way so we can live another day.

Yet, it is just as important for us to understand and accept that we are not protected from danger or afforded the opportunity to run and hide in every situation. Hebrews 11:1-35 offers a riveting review of acts of supernatural faith, divine power, protection, deliverance, and intervention. As the pace of the commentary quickens, we are carried towards the climax in verses 32-40 where the narrator juxtaposes the feats of persons like Gideon, Barak, Sampson, Jephthae, David, and Samuel with "others" in Hebrews 11:35-37:

*Women received their dead raised to life again: and others were tortured, not accepting deliverance; that they might obtain a better resurrection: And others had trial of cruel mockings and scourgings, yea, moreover of bonds and imprisonment: They were stoned, they were sawn asunder, were tempted, were slain with the sword: they wandered about in sheepskins and goatskins, being destitute, afflicted, tormented.*

The "and others" of verse 35 who did not escape the edge of the sword are part of the same glorious procession of victors who through faith obtained a good report!

This thought is also highlighted in the encounter recorded in Daniel 3 between Shadrach, Meshach and Abednego, in their dialogue with Nebuchadnezzar, king of Babylon.

These three young men faced an enraged king and a fiery furnace so hot that it slew the men who eventually threw them into the furnace for refusing to bow down to the image the king had erected. They responded to the king's edict and threat with this confident assertion:

*We are not careful to answer thee in this matter. If it be so, our God whom we serve is able to deliver us from the burning fiery furnace, and he will deliver us out of thine hand, O king. But if not, be it known unto thee, O king, that we will not serve thy gods, not worship the golden image which thou hast set up. (Daniel 3:16-18)*

In his wrath, Nebuchadnezzar had put this question to them *(Daniel 3:15)*: *"Who is that God that shall deliver you out of my hands?"* The response of these young men was not rash youthful defiance, but a thoughtful, intentional declaration of the ability and power of their God to deliver them from the fiery furnace.

But what is even more fascinating was their unequivocal acquiescence to God's sovereignty. The strength, courage, and confidence of these men lay in their calm assurance that their God could deliver them from the burning fiery furnace, and that whether or not He delivered them from the furnace, *"he will deliver us out of thine hand, O king" (Daniel 3:17)*.

The words of the three Hebrew boys are indeed compelling. Shadrach, Meshach, and Abednego were unambiguous and unequivocal in their belief and purpose. They were prepared and ready to lay down their lives on the veracity of God's ability to deliver them out of the fiery furnace, but if not, they avowed that they would still not bow down to the king's image which he had set up.

*"But if not"* did not limit God, and was not an expression of doubt. Rather, these words demonstrated their understanding that God's ways and purposes are always higher and His plans so superior to ours that our finite minds may never be able to fully comprehend them.

These men knew and understood that finite men should dare not dictate to God nor predict or presume on His behalf. But they knew that whatever happened – whether God delivered them from the fiery furnace or not – they would be "protected." Their protection and deliverance was secure for they would be "delivered" out of the hands of the king into the almighty hands of their God.

They were never in the king's hand in any case.

*"For whether we live therefore, or die, we are the Lord's" (Romans 14:8).*

Naboth, in 1 Kings 21, is someone who did not escape the edge of the sword. Innocent, wrongly accused, seeking only to defend his family's patrimony, Naboth faced the cruel fury of Jezebel and was mercilessly executed so that her childish, avaricious, cowardly husband could seize and take over his vineyard.

John the Baptist was beheaded, as was James. Stephen, the first Christian martyr, was stoned to death, falsely accused of speaking blasphemous words against Moses and against God.

Even when the lives of many of these men of God were spared, they were not exempt from affliction, hardship, and adversity. Daniel was thrown into the den of lions. Peter was arrested, chained, and handed over to sixteen soldiers to be executed the following day. Jeremiah the prophet was imprisoned and put in stocks for speaking forth God's truth. And take a look at Paul's bio:

> *Of the Jews received I forty stripes save one. Thrice was I beaten with rods, once was I stoned, thrice I suffered shipwreck, a night and a day I have been in the deep; in journeyings often, in perils in waters, in perils of robbers, in perils by mine own countrymen, in perils by the heathen, in perils in the city, in perils in the wilderness, in perils in the sea, in perils among false brethren; in weariness and painfulness, in watchings often, in, in hunger and thirst, in fastings often, in cold and nakedness. (2 Corinthians 11:24-28)*

Some twentieth century martyrs who captured my interest during my teens were five missionaries who, sensing the call of God upon their lives, ventured into the rain forests of Ecuador to share the gospel of Jesus Christ with the Auca Indians – a tribe that at that time was completely isolated from the outside world and were known to be warlike, fierce, and hostile to strangers.

As a teenager, I read the books my mother had in her collection about their lives and deaths, Jungle Pilot by Russell T. Hitt, and Through Gates of Splendour by Elisabeth Elliot. These men – Jim Elliot, Nate Saint, Ed MacCully, Peter Fleming, and Roger Youderian – left the comfort of their families and homes because they believed that the whole world needed to hear the gospel of Jesus Christ – including the Aucas.

In 1956, following several overtures of friendship and goodwill towards the Aucas, all five missionaries were speared to death in their camp in the Amazon rain forests.

Today, these five men are among the "and others" in that great march of victors, that great cloud of witnesses of Hebrews 11 who were stoned, or tortured, or sawn asunder , suffered scourging and cruel mocking. They did not accept deliverance that they might obtain a better resurrection.

## CHERITH – PLACE OF REST AND SOLITUDE

*"Turn thee eastward, and hide thyself…" (1 Kings17:3).*

Cherith was also the place where Elijah was given "time out." After the prophet had made his pronouncement to Ahab, God immediately commanded him to go into retreat. God did not allow the prophet to occupy a front row seat to observe how God fulfilled His word. He was asked to step back, step aside, to rest…

Elijah's meeting with Ahab, and his pronouncement of divine punishment would have been highly emotional and conflicting. God's solution was simple, "Come apart, Elijah, rest awhile, by yourself." In his book, *The Hidden Link Between Adrenalin and Stress*, Dr. Archibald D. Hart observes that for his own well-being, as soon as possible after the emergency, a person needs to bring down the level of arousal and move back to a non-emergency mode.[1]

Medical and health science corroborate this. For our good health and well-being, we all need "down time" – time to recover, to refocus, to regroup. Although he was a powerful prophet of God, Elijah was yet only human. He needed time for recovery following his confrontation with Ahab and Jezebel. God, the Creator of the universe, the one who made man in His own image, knew that the prophet needed to rest and relax in solitude. "Come apart, Elijah, rest a while, by yourself."

There was another person of the Godhead who understood the importance of this rest and solitude. Quiet time alone with His Father was a priority with Him. In Mark 1:35-39, after ministering to the entire city of Galilee which had gathered by the door of Peter's house, and after healing many that were sick and demon-possessed, Jesus got up early in the morning and departed into a solitary place to pray. Just after John the Baptist was killed, Jesus told His disciples, *"Come ye apart into a desert place and rest a while" (Mark 6:31-32).* The death of John the Baptist would have been a highly emotional experience both for Jesus and His disciples. They needed time out. That evening found Jesus alone on the mountain, waiting in prayer all night.

Quiet time alone can renew us. It benefits body, mind, and spirit, and is espe-cially essential after emotional highs. Oftentimes, as believers and followers of

Jesus Christ, we find ourselves driven to do, prove, perform, and seek approval. We allow ourselves to be pushed – sometimes by our own inner selves, sometimes by others – into engaging in every battle, fighting every wrong, seeing to every need, attending every meeting, and taking care of every detail. As a result, we never refresh ourselves physically, mentally, emotionally, or spiritually. We burn out.

*But there is a rest in this very life that belongs to the people of God.*

Gordon Macdonald suggests that joylessness and lack of vitality in the Christian life can be a result of this type of "driven" lifestyle. In his very instructive book, *Ordering Your Private World*, he observes, "A restless work style produces a restless person. Work that goes on month after month without a genuine pause to inquire of its meaning... will drain the private world of vitality and joy." [2]

All of us need a place of rest and solitude – to think, evaluate, pray, and meditate... or to just "be." It could be one day in every week, or several moments in a day. Look at the times in His short three and a half years of ministry when Jesus found a solitary place to pray and listen to His Father... alone. We do not need to be driven by the demands of life, or by others for their approval or commendation – no matter how significant they may be in our lives. Jesus says that when we come to Him, heavy laden, laboring, He will give rest. He invites us, one and all, to take *His* yoke on us – not the yoke of life, or of other persons, or causes (no matter how noble they might be) – but *His* yoke. When we do we will find rest for our souls because *His* yoke is easy and *His* burden is light (Matthew 11:28-30).

*"In quietness and confidence shall be your strength" (Isaiah 30:15).*

## CHERITH – PLACE OF PROMISE

*"Thou shalt drink of the brook; and I have commanded the ravens to feed thee there" (1 Kings 17:4).*

Cherith represented God's promise to sustain the prophet during the drought. Elijah would drink water from the brook and God would send the ravens to feed him. Elijah believed God. The account states that he went and did according to the word of the Lord, *"for he went and dwelt by the brook Cherith, that is before Jordan" (1 Kings 17:5).*

Did God fulfill His promise to the prophet? Indeed. First Kings 17:6 says that the ravens brought him bread and flesh in the morning and bread and flesh in the evening, and he drank of the brook. God promised Elijah that in this time of drought in the nation of Israel he would be provided for and sustained at the brook Cherith. Elijah believed God's promise and acted upon the promise in faith. *He went and did according to the word of the Lord. The fulfillment of the promise was contingent upon Elijah's faith in God's promise and also his obedience to God's directives.*

Faith and obedience.

The Bible is a book of promises. We live the Christian life based on the promise that if any man comes to Christ, he will never be turned away and that when we come to Christ we become new persons. The Holy Spirit of God comes to live within us and empowers us to live a new kind of life because Christ died for our sins according to the Scriptures. Through His death and resurrection, we have eternal life (1 Corinthians 15:1-5).

## The Promises of God

We believe that we have eternal life because of the promises of God. *"He that believeth on me though he were dead, yet shall he live" (John 11:25-26).*

We believe that we have a home in heaven based on the promises of God. *"I go to prepare a place for you... and I will come again to receive you unto myself that where I am there ye may be also" (John 14:1-4).*

This requires faith. The Christian life cannot be lived without faith. Without faith it is impossible to please God, *"for he that cometh to God must believe that He is and that He is the rewarder of those who diligently seek Him" (Hebrews 11:6).*

Promises. Faith. Without these we have no Christian life. We have no hope of life in Heaven after this life. We have absolutely no hope in this life, nor the one to come.

Are God's promises reliable? Can we "stand" on these promises? Can we lay our stake on them?

The Scripture tells us that the promises of God in Christ are yea, and in Him, amen… unto the glory of God. In other words, God's promises are to be trusted. He does not go back on His Word (2 Corinthians 1:20). Psalm 138:2 says that God magnifies His Word above His name. In Jeremiah 1:12, the Lord told Jeremiah that He is watching over His Word to make sure that it is fulfilled.

The Bible assures us that we can rest upon the promises of God. What does God promise? He promises us, among other things:

- *Salvation*, if we believe on the Lord Jesus Christ (Acts12:31, Romans 10:13).
- *Eternal life*. That's why Jesus came and died (John 3:16).
- A home with Him in Heaven (John 14:1-4).
- Christ will return to earth for His children; those who have died and those who are still alive (1 Thessalonians 4:14-18).
- Daily provision for our daily needs, if we seek the things of His Kingdom first (Matthew 6:19-34).
- Answers to our prayers (Mark 11:24, Matthew 7:7-1, Philippians 4:6-7).
- His watchful care over us in this life (2 Chronicles 16:9, Psalm 34:15, 1 Peter 5:7).
- To be with us always, never ever leaving us or forsaking us (Hebrews 13:5, Matthew 28:20).
- Nothing and no one can separate us from His love (Romans 8:38-39).
- He is for us – on our side (Romans 8:31-37).
- We are more than conquerors (Romans 8:37).

We must have faith to obey and act upon the Word of God. We must believe. We must trust and we must obey. Hebrews 3 and 4:1-11 recount the reasons why an entire generation of Israelites did not enter into the promised land of rest, but rather perished in the wilderness. The reason is offered in verse 2 of chapter 4: *"The word preached did not profit them, not being mixed with faith in them that heard it."*

We are saved by faith, and we live this Christian life also by faith. As we have received the Lord Jesus Christ, even so we must walk in Him – not by sight but by faith (2 Corinthians 5:7).

Without faith it is *impossible* to please God.

It is faith in God which makes us able to stand on His Word, trust in His Word, rely upon His Word, obey His precepts and instructions, and persevere to the end.

*Faith – a gift from God. The gift we all need most. We need faith to believe the promises, to stand on the promises, and to wait for the promises, even though they may be long in coming.*

*We need faith to trust and obey.*

## CHERITH – PLACE OF PROVISION

As noted earlier, what God promised to Elijah happened just as He said. Elijah drank each day from this brook, and every morning and evening the provision of bread and flesh was airlifted to him via ravens.

### Natural Provision

Cherith was strategically selected. Elijah needed water in order to survive. He needed an isolated place where he would not be easily found, and he needed solitude to recuperate, recreate, rest, and be strengthened.

The account states that Elijah went and dwelt by the brook and drank from it. The brook was a tributary of the river Jordan. There was nothing supernatural about the place; it was just a natural brook flowing with water. God did not make the brook flow with water for the prophet – it was a flowing brook long before God told Elijah to go there. Elijah just needed to get there and drink from the brook for his daily sustenance.

Cherith provided the protection, solitude, isolation, and sustenance the prophet needed at the time.

God is sovereign, and He can use natural means to provide for His people, and in fact, for every living creature on the earth. He sends rain on the just and the unjust (Matthew 5:45). He forms light and He forms darkness. The fowl of the air do not sow nor reap, but God provides for them day by day as He does for the lilies of the field.

When Joshua led the people of Israel to conquer the land of promise, their first combat zone was Jericho. The men who were sent to spy out the land lodged in Rahab's house. She was a prostitute, and we know that God used her to help deliver that city to His people.

## Supernatural Provision

But Cherith was also the place of supernatural provision. Ravens, at the command of God, arrived morning and evening with bread and flesh for the prophet. We first read about the raven in the book of Genesis. After the flood rains subside, Noah opens the window of the ark and sends forth a raven, which we are told went to and fro until the waters were dried up from the earth.

There are several significant things to note about ravens:

- They are regarded as the world's smartest birds.
- They are migratory birds.
- They are carrion eaters, regarded as scavengers and as a result, unclean animals.

It is the raven that God decided to use to send with bread and flesh for Elijah every morning and every night – a bird that is unclean and feeds on the meat of dead animals! A most unlikely choice, one would think.

Every morning and every evening, this bird – a scavenging, migratory, unclean bird – flew its way to Elijah with bread and flesh on the instructions of His Heavenly Father.

I recall many years ago when I was studying for an MPhil in Spanish at the University of the West Indies in Jamaica. My area of research was Puerto Rican Nationalist Theater. My supervisor and head of the Spanish Department, Dr. George Irish, arranged for me to be awarded a six-week scholarship to Puerto Rico where I was able to do field work and research. One of the authors I studied was the very well-known Puerto Rican dramatist, Rene Marquez.

One day, after receiving instructions on how to reach him and making an appointment with him, I headed out for our meeting. He lived way out in the country. I arrived at the house which I thought to be his, only to find that I had gone to the wrong place. The gentleman at this house was a Mr. Marques, but he was not the playwright with whom I had the appointment. He had heard of Mr. Marquez and told me how to get to his home. By this time it was much too late to continue the journey, so I returned to San Juan, annoyed that I had wasted so much time for nothing.

A few days later, having called and apologized, I headed out again for my appointment with Rene Marquez. This time, I was successful. He lived very, very far out, and after the bus dropped me off, I still had a very long walk to get to his house. I interviewed him and chatted with him about Puerto Rican nationalist theater, and after a few hours, left for San Juan.

I got out to the main road and waited for the bus to arrive. It was then about five in the afternoon. I waited and waited, but no bus arrived. I became very worried and anxious. I was way out in the country in Puerto Rico, and I did not see many people who looked like me.

It slowly began to get dark, and by that time I was in total panic. I was afraid, not knowing what to do, nor where to go for help.

Just at that time a car passed me, reversed, and then stopped beside me. The driver opened the door and beckoned me. To my surprise, it was the man whose house I had visited in error two afternoons before. He asked me where I was going and I told him that I was waiting for the bus. What he said almost took my breath away. He informed me that buses stopped running in this area at 4 in the afternoon. He had seen me standing there as he passed by me, and recognized me as the young lady who came by his house by mistake two days before. He knew I was a stranger here and surmised I did not know the buses were no longer running in this area. He put his car in reverse, came back to me, and drove me all the way to San Juan. I was able to catch a bus there that brought me all the way to the house where I was staying.

I recalled the day I thought I had "wasted" going to this man's house. I was so upset and disgruntled that I had wasted that day. But on that evening, when he met me waiting for a bus which would have never come, I knew that it was all God's plan of provision – *divine provision put in place in advance*. I couldn't bear to think about what would have ensued had I not "wasted" that day and gone to his house in error.

I related this experience to a gentleman I met on a flight from Jamaica to Puerto Rico. His only response was, *"And they say there is no God."*

God can use anyone and anything in His providence and in His deter-mination to provide for His children. We are not the ones who make that decision. It is all God's.

The widow woman in 2 Kings 4 was on the verge of losing her two sons as slaves to her creditors. In desperation she went to Elijah for assistance. She needed divine intervention. Elijah simply asked her, "What hast thou in thy house?" The pot of oil and some borrowed empty vessels become the instruments of miraculous provision!

I will always remember an elderly Pentecostal preacher recounting God's amazing provision for him and his family. In his day, the ministry was not a lucrative vocation. Most ministers of the gospel lived by faith – really and truly trusting God to provide one day at a time. He spoke of having no money to buy food for his family. On one such occasion, feeling somewhat desperate, he walked to a nearby dry river bed and began praying to God for help. As he prayed he heard a voice saying to him, "Look down." He did and then saw a brand new shilling on the ground beside his foot. It was more than enough to supply food for his family for many days!

God provides. But more amazing are the means that God uses, which we would normally overlook or despise: a pot of oil, an unclean bird, a prosti-tute, a wasted day...

## CHERITH – A DRIED-UP BROOK

Cherith, the place of protection, solitude, promise, and provision, became the place where God's promised provision eventually evaporated and dried up.

Does God's provision dry up?

Read the account. It states that *"after a while, the brook dried up because there had been no rain in the land" (1 Kings 17:7).*

God's provision dried up. The brook Cherith, where God told Elijah to go and promised to sustain him, dried up.

Our view of the incident is twenty-twenty hindsight. We know how the story ends. Elijah would not have known how the incident would unfold – just like Job didn't. We have no idea how much time passed between verse 7 and verse 8 of 1 Kings 17. We do not know if Elijah went without food and water for a day, two days, three days, or even more. We have no way of knowing.

Did Elijah panic? Did he become worried and anxious? Was he tempted to doubt? Did he ever wonder what games God was playing with him? Do you think Elijah expected the brook to continue to flow miraculously and thus felt as if a cruel joke had been played on him?

We are given no answers to these questions. We can surmise that as the days passed, Elijah noticed at first that the waters of Cherith were subsiding, then that they had been reduced to just a trickle, and finally stopped altogether.

He would have watched as God's promised provision for his sustenance depleted!

As stated earlier, implicit in the account is the idea that the drought was God's way of punishing an idolatrous Israel. *The Harper Collins Study Bible* tells us that according to the mythology of the Baal cult, the storm god was responsible for bringing life-giving rains at certain times of the year and thus restoring fertility to the land. After the yearly rainy season, the ground got progressively drier, and eventually all vegetation died. During this period, Baal was thought to be in the power of the god of death and sterility. [3]

In stating, *"As the Lord lives and according to my word" (1 Kings 17:1),* Elijah was announcing that the yearly alternation between life and death was an illusion and that Baal had nothing to do with bringing rain and fertility. He was demonstrating to the people that the Lord controls rain and drought, fertility and sterility, and life and death. He illustrated this by announcing that God had decreed a three year drought.

The New Testament book of James, chapter 5, gives further insight. It informs us that Elijah prayed fervently that it might not rain, and for three years and six months no rain came. *Elijah and God were working together in this.*

Elijah was faithful to God even at a time when many had turned their backs on true worship and were incorporating the mythology of Baal's cult into the worship of God. As a true prophet of God, he must have been sorely grieved by this situation and therefore prayed that God would not send rain and show to these people that He, Jehovah, was the only true God.

Elijah was God's prophet who spoke on God's behalf. He was an obedient and faithful servant of God. God promised him that He would provide for him at Cherith by sending ravens to feed him morning and night, and by letting the brook provide him with drinking water. This happened for some time, but *"it came to pass after a while, that the brook dried up, because there had been no rain in the land" (1 Kings 17:7).*

Elijah had put himself on the line for God. He had placed himself in phys-ical danger by confronting Ahab. He had been a faithful and obedient prophet in the face of idolatry and apostasy rampant in the land. God told him He would provide for him at Cherith – yet God's provision for him dried up.

What happens when God's provision dries up? It did for Elijah, Job, and Job's wife...

Is it right or okay to feel afraid, embarrassed, bitter, or resentful? Is it okay to wonder what you did wrong – to engage in introspection and self-searching? Is it right or okay to feel disappointed with God and even angry with Him? Are such emotions sacrilegious? Do they border on heresy?

Is it sinful to blame God... and to feel that maybe you have been serving Him in vain? Does God forgive such thoughts and actions against Him? Does He understand? Does He care?

Sometimes God can seem ruthless in His determination to carry through His plan, yet we are unable to see what the plan is. Our brook has dried up and we have nowhere else to turn, so we plead and cry for help like Joseph in the prison in Egypt. But does God answer? No. The door is closed tight and impenetrable. Not even a face is looking through the window in acknowledgment.

For some it is the brook of a cherished relationship – a once loving, close, and cherished relationship with a spouse or a best friend. You might have felt certain that this was a match made in Heaven and that God brought you together. You saw God's hand of provision in your union or your friendship. It could not have happened to you unless it was the hand of God – His divine provision and providence.

Now all love and caring is gone – dried up. All that's left is the dry bed of bitterness, resentment, betrayal, mistrust, and hurt. To your consternation and utter amazement, the love and caring did not last. You saw it slow to a trickle, and then waited with pounding heart and baited breath for the flow to resurge. You thought this could not be happening to you. You did all you could. But it dried up...

This is the experience of many of God's beloved sons and daughters. Many of God's children have found themselves here, at this brook. Dried up... no love left. Dried up. They entered into a marriage relationship with a Christian brother or sister feeling certain to have been in God's will, only to find the brook go dry. Nothing left but memories – many of them bitter and filled with regret. I know of those who prayed and fasted, who felt drawn to sacrificial service and giving to God, expecting in return that the brook would begin to flow again, that the hurt, pain, and disappointment would go away and the friendship and harmony would return. It just didn't happen.

In fact, for some there seemed to have been a light in the window, some drawing of the curtain, a hope that, yes, my prayers are working, only to have all hopes crushed… again, with feelings even worse than before. The brook of love and friendship dried up. Someone who experienced such a dried-up brook said to me some time ago: "To have gone into a marriage which ended in failure is a tragedy, such is my belief in the institution which God has ordained. It will remain an unresolved issue to my grave, even though I feel that God in His mercy delivered me…"

Does it mean that God did not provide the brook in the first place? These are the existential questions that can torment and afflict the believer. *I married in the faith,* you say to yourself. *I was not unequally yoked with an ungodly spouse.* You see others who did not obey God like you did, still married – happily – and wonder where your marriage went wrong. What did I do wrong? *Perhaps I should have… Perhaps I shouldn't have…*

Are you here, at this brook right now?

Perhaps your dried-up brook is a matter of health. You and your loved ones felt blessed with good health. But without any warning and through no fault of your own, it was taken away. The brook of health evaporated, leaving the scars of illness in your family. You took good care of yourself, followed the rules of dietary health and fitness, and still disease invaded and ravaged your body.

Have you been there, at this brook?

They tell you that you should not be sick, that God wants us well. You pray and you believe with all the fervor and faith that you have, but nothing changes. You have been struck down. Your brook of health has dried up. You agonize when you hear the platitudes and glib comments of the "health and wealth" Christians who seem to have it all together.

*What is wrong with me?* you ask yourself.

*Have you been there? Are you still there at this dried-up brook?*

Some of you reading this book have seen your finances diminish. You have lost your job. You have tried everything and anything and nothing has worked. You have been living on the brink for years, terrified that one day you will fall over the precipice. You now have no savings (depleted long ago), no pension, no hope for anything good to happen… no future as you see it. Nothing. Just a dried-up brook.

Many televangelists proclaim that such financial struggles should not happen to God's children. That if it does happen and does not change, then it must be some curse, something you are not doing right, or you are not giving enough – you need to give more, believe more, trust more, give more, give them more…

Since it works for those on television and God provides without fail in abundance for them, giving them luxury cars and private jets and the ability to stay in the most expensive hotels in London, Paris, and New York, you ask yourself: What is wrong with me?

In your desperation you follow the advice and give more and more to them… but bills continue to mount up. The creditors threaten you. At times you actually feel as if you have no one to turn to. And how can you turn to anyone anyway? You are embarrassed, disappointed, ashamed that you – one who has served God all your life, never turned away from Him, always striven to please and glorify Him – find yourself in this rut, this financial drought.

A new day becomes a frightening specter, not a challenge or a hope for change. In fact, you always feel afraid. But you are too afraid to tell anyone that you are afraid, so you keep it to yourself. But it is wearing you down.

*You are experiencing financial dry times…*

*"I wish above all things that you would prosper and be in health, even as your soul prospers…"(3 John 2).* You ask yourself over and over if this Scripture applies to you. You search yourself. You agonize…

*What did I do wrong? What have I done wrong? What am I doing wrong?*

You begin to lose your confidence in God and in yourself. You begin not to expect anything. It's just a joke. (Expecting something good to happen, I mean.)

Your waking hours are spent worrying about your future, about how you will make it. How will you provide for yourself and your family? How long before everyone finds out and your life becomes an open reproach? Pride has reared its head and drains you even further.

At times life seems more like hell.

What did my parents teach me? Is it really true? Is it all a myth, a fable?

*"I was young and now I am old and yet I have never seen the righteous forsaken nor his seed begging bread" (Psalm 37:35).* But you feel forsaken.

He is not listening. He has not listened for some time now. He has not come through for you.

Hanging by a thread. Every day... hanging by a thread.

All the things that should help you haunt you. You try and try and try because you are committed to your family. But it just does not work out. You've tried everything. Nothing seems to work. Financial dry times. Protracted. Ongoing. No hope in view.

Are you there at this moment in your life? Have you ever been there? I know some who have been and are still there. It happens to people who love and serve God and try to please Him. And it can go on and on and on – almost as if there is no end in view.

Five? Ten... more years of financial struggles, financial drought? Dry times happen, even to believing, obedient Christians who give and serve God, and are faithful to Him.

I once heard a young man giving part of a very touching testimony at a church. He later shared it with me for this book. He graduated from college with a diploma in Electrical Engineering (Electronics and Telecommunication). Because of the continuing volcanic crisis in Montserrat, he decided to move to the United Kingdom where, after some time, he was able to secure a very lucrative job in a company. In addition, he was quickly promoted. His salary allowed for a comfortable lifestyle and he and his wife were soon able to purchase their own car, a family home, and then two other homes. They took annual vacations. Life was very good. They were able to share their material blessings with others who were in need.

But the brook dried up. Some nine years later, he was given notice that he was to be laid off. He felt numb and shortchanged by his employers – somewhat like a spurned lover. He felt he had given so much to the company and was devastated to find that he was facing unemployment because it was downsizing. The law required the company to provide him with thirty days of counseling, but he felt so detached from the company that he stopped showing up for it, deciding he did not want any intermediary help. He asked to be immediately let go. He had to sign a paper releasing the company from any liability. He did this. He felt that he knew what he was doing.

But it was all downhill from there on. His savings dried up quickly because he was unable to get another job. The Department of Social Services gave him only £67 per week. At his old job, his taxes alone were almost £2000 monthly!

His wife decided to increase her working hours to help after he was taken to the courts twice for repossession of their home. Cupboards usually stocked with food were empty. The children, unaccustomed to this kind of life, began to complain.

He told me he felt abandoned by God. He would question God over and over: Why did this happen? What did I do wrong? Why did you build me up and now knock me down? There were more questions than answers.

Prayer became a one-way conversation. He was doing all the talking – just trying to get some answers. There were times when he felt he could not pray, but he asked others to pray for him.

Many times, he came close to giving up. He said he felt less than a man – unable to support his family. One day, in a car park on the roof of a building, looking down, he heard a voice whispering, telling him to throw himself down and end it all. His children were in the car and he looked at them and thought about how they would feel if he left them in that way.

When arguments would develop at home about him not having a job or about money, he would think about ending it all. "Looking at train tracks and wanting to jump is a real feeling I experienced a few times," he said. "I also felt being dead would be better than what I was facing."

*His brook had dried up. Or so it seemed...*

There were believers in Israel at the time of Elijah's drought. Some 7,000 of them who had not bowed their knees to Baal, "nor kissed his mouth." Do you think they were spared the consequences of the drought because they were believers?

Perhaps because of the disappointments and difficulties, the twists and unexpected turns you've faced in life, your faith and trust in God have just about dried up. Perhaps it is something so unmentionable and unspeakable that you keep it all inside. You no longer have hope. Not much anyway. If anything... it's just a trickle. You smile and bear your burdens alone while your heart might be bleeding inside.

You pretend that all is well even though you are filled with fear and anxiety. You continue to attend a church, which does not in any way minister to you. You have the sense that your faith in a good God who is willing to come to the help of His people is dissipating, slowly, ever so slowly, day by day, through experience after experience...

You feel disillusioned. You feel fear. You feel that life is slipping away through your fingers. You feel helpless to stop it.

You have no more expectations. Better not to expect anything than to be disappointed. You are tired of being disappointed... and you are angry.

Really, what do you do when you have done everything you have been told and taught to do and life still is not working for you? What do you do when the foundations are shaken? What do you do when what you relied on for your sustenance, the promises you believed in, the faith you laid claim to all seem to evaporate?

What do you do when you have prayed, believed, obeyed, and faithfully followed God, yet your life is just one impassable mountain after the other, one uncrossable river after the next, one unfulfilled promise after another, mirages in your wilderness of bewilderment – when there no clouds of rain in sight, not even the size of the fist of a man?

What do you do when your brook has dried up and there is no rain in sight and many years have passed, yet you have not gotten to Zarephath?

Have you ever been there? Are you still there – *at a dried-up brook?*

# Chapter 4

## Lessons from Cherith

*"The judgments of the Lord*
*are true and righteous altogether."*
*Psalm 19:9b*

**Brooks Serving Obedient, Faithful Men and Women of God Do Dry Up.**

One of the obvious lessons we garner from the account in 1 Kings 17 is that it is not just the brooks of the disobedient, rebellious, and wayward which dry up. Brooks can dry up even when we are obedient to God's commands and are living in His perfect will. Brooks can dry up even though God is leading and guiding our lives and we are living in His favor.

People who serve God faithfully may not necessarily be spared from the problems and difficulties that confront others who do not regard God in their hearts. Asaph, in pondering this issue, spoke of the spiritual and emotional dilemma he faced when he attempted to compare the lot of the righteous man with that of the ungodly. He could not help but note the apparent ease with which the ungodly seemed to be able to live their lives and flourish. His perspective was improved – greatly improved – by attending church. He went into the sanctuary of the Lord, listened to the Word of God, and was reminded of God's righteous judgments and the immutability of His promises (Psalm 73:17).

Even when God used His prophet Elijah to foretell His judgment against the land of Israel and its idolatrous king and inhabitants, this did not preclude the prophet from experiencing the problems that accompany such a national crisis. We do not know how soon after the brook dried up that Elijah was told to go to Zarephath. We do not know if he had several days of waiting without water or food before God told him what to do and what He had prepared for him. We do know that God sent him to Cherith to be provided for and sustained, and that Cherith dried up.

Sometimes, unfortunately, current religious trends make it immensely difficult for the Christian whose brook has dried up to openly share his experience with other Christians. Prosperity, good health, education, and wealth are paraded in our pulpits everywhere as the entitlement of every born-again believer. Those who find that life is not working for them at any point in time are often left to feel that something must be wrong with them – some sin, some error. Or worse yet – that God is not just. He is not fair.

Today, ministers of the gospel tell us to claim it and it is ours. "Sow your seed – preferably *into my ministry* – and the more you sow the more you will reap in wealth and health," they preach. Doubtless many have sown and reaped. But for as many as have sown and reaped, countless others have sown, named it and claimed it, believed, trusted, fasted, prayed, spoken the word of faith, and yet continue to sit beside a dried-up brook.

*Brooks can dry up even when we are obedient to God's commands and are living in His perfect will.*

Does this mean we should not engage in self-searching at such times?

Absolutely not. Self-searching and self-examination are fundamental to every believer's walk and growth. We need to practice self-searching when certain situations happen or are prolonged in our lives. There are sufficient examples in the Bible which suggest that we reap what we sow, and that very often when bad things happen it can be as a consequence of our own wrong-doing and disobedience. After all, as we have already seen, the drought in Israel during the reign of Ahab was mainly a punishment for the idolatry of the children of Israel and their rebellion against the laws of God.

In 1 Corinthians 11, Paul admonished believers to examine themselves when they came together to observe the sacrament of the Lord's Supper. *"But let a man examine himself, and so let him eat of that bread, and drink of that cup" (1 Corinthians 11:28).* Self-examination, the passage suggests, can prevent the believer from taking the sacraments unworthily and suffering serious consequences. *"For this cause many are weak and sickly among you and many sleep..." (1 Corinthians 11:30).*

As a young person, I recall members of the Pentecostal church in which I grew up took this admonition seriously and literally. Just before the Lord's Supper was served, a sister might approach another with whom she had some form of dispute. Both would leave the church building and remain outside until they resolved the disagreement. Only then would they return to partake of the Lord's Supper.

Perhaps some of you reading have such memories. My father, the pastor of the church, was unwavering in his teaching that it was just as dangerous to stay away from the Lord's Table as it was to take the emblems unworthily. The solution was self-examination.

*"For if we would judge ourselves we should not be judged" (1 Corinthians 11:31).*

The story of Samson in the book of Judges 13-16 illustrates the life of a man whose brooks all dried up because of lustful self-indulgence. He eventually found himself bound with fetters of brass, grinding in the prison house of the Philistines, eyes gouged out, his amazing strength gone, his prominence and tenure as a judge in Israel all a thing of the past. Why? Because throughout his life, he insisted on making self-centered choices all aimed at gratifying his lust and selfish desires.

Here was a man of special birth – like Isaac or John the Baptist, blessed by God and ordained to "begin to deliver Israel from the hands of the Philistines" (Judges 13:5). He was a miracle child, foretold to his parents in a most supernatural manner, born with divine purpose and intention. But his eyes were one of his greatest setbacks. They were lustful and covetous eyes, and he had to have what or whoever he saw and wanted. This man who judged Israel for twenty years, whose birth was so special that an angel came to announce it to his parents – ended up a laughingstock, an object of derision for the enemies of God – the Philistines. He gave "great occasion to the enemies of God to blaspheme" (2 Samuel 12:14), for as they looked at Samson and talked about him, they sacrificed to Dagon their god and rejoiced because **"our god hath delivered Samson our enemy into our hands" (Judges 16:23-24).**

But Samson got an opportunity to examine himself. In prison and blind, he was no longer distracted by his eyes. His strength, prominence, and distinction had all dried up. Gone was the brawn and bravura, showmanship, and self-gratification. All that was left was reliance on God, the God who had endowed him with the strength he had. For the first time, we hear Samson praying, calling upon this God:

*"O Lord God, remember me, I pray thee and strengthen me, I pray thee, only this once, that I may be avenged of the Philistines for my two eyes" (Judges 16:28).*

God answered his prayer.

*Self-searching is an essential spiritual discipline.* Nonetheless, we need divine wisdom from God so as not to wallow in this exercise.

Psalm 139:23-24 advocates the highest form of self-searching – the kind which allows God to guide us through the exercise of it, for so very often we have secret faults within us and don't even fully understand our errors (Psalm 19:12). If God, through the prompting of the Holy Spirit and the revealed Word, reminds us of any sin or infractions in our lives, it is important that we deal with them as David did in Psalm 51. We serve a God who is *"faithful and just to forgive us our sins and to cleanse us from all unrighteousness" (1 John 1:9).* But if there is no such prompting, we should be careful not to let the accuser of the brethren turn all our actions into felonious and iniquitous wrongdoing.

There is nothing to be gained from living out our spiritual lives in incessant flagellation of ourselves.

A dried-up brook is not necessarily the consequence of sin and wrongdoing. Elijah brought the word of God's divine judgment to Ahab and the inhabitants of the land. Elijah stood up and stood out for the right. Elijah was among those who served the true God faithfully and refused to be quiet in the face of the blatant idolatry of his people.

Elijah confronted the most fearful and formidable of foes in his day – Jezebel. God sent him to the brook Cherith. He told Elijah that he would be fed there, he would drink from the brook and ravens would feed him. Did Elijah ever imagine that his brook would dry up? I would rather think that he believed that perhaps, in some miraculous way, God would keep the water running in this brook for the entire tenure of the drought. But *"it came to pass after a while, that the brook dried up, because there had been no rain in the land" (1 Kings 17:7).*

Asaph, Elijah, and Job all faced dried-up brooks, as did Joseph and Paul the Apostle. You are in good company. Job's friends who came to mourn with him and comfort him ended up accusing him of all kinds of wrongdoing against God. *"Remember, I pray thee, who ever perished, being innocent? Or where were the righteous cut off?" (Job 4:7), said one, while another taunted: "If thou wert pure and upright: surely now [God] would awake for thee..." (Job 8:7).* Another advised him, *"If iniquity be in thine hand, put it far away, and let not wickedness dwell in thy tabernacles" (Job 11:14).*

The arguments of Job's friends may sound reasonable and judicious, but these men were wrong in their conclusions about God and Job, and in their assessment of the reason for Job's suffering. God became angry with them for the accusations they leveled against Job because they had not spoken the things which were right (Job 42:7).

The Scripture is clear. Brooks have dried up for many of God's choicest and beloved children who have been obedient and faithful followers of the Lord.

## When We Are Battered by Life Experiences, It Is Human to Feel Baffled

There are many emotions which can accompany baffling life experiences, like that of a dried-up brook. Depression, doubt, anxiety, fear, and panic are common and universal responses.

A dried-up brook is a place where God's promises and provision have seemingly been exhausted, dissipated, or disappeared. It can represent a place where hope and expectation are lost and despair, doubt, fear, and panic can become tyrannical masters.

A dried-up brook is a crisis situation because it creates a feeling of risk, the feeling of being in a hazardous situation. It is a crisis because it is involuntary and out of the person's control. It is overwhelming and extraordinary and it is a crisis because the questions "when," "how," "how long," "to what extent," and "what will happen after" seem unanswerable.

To feel safe and secure is a basic human need. Dried-up brooks can make a person feel unsafe, and cause them to lose confidence in the world as an ordered, secure, and reliable place. The result of this can be fear. People who face dried-up brooks can find themselves paralyzed by fear and panic, and unable to move forward.

Fear can be a debilitating and traumatizing emotion to deal with.

Franklin D Roosevelt, a president of the United States is quoted as saying, *"there is nothing to fear but fear itself."*

I do not think the Bible agrees with him. The many references in the scriptures which admonish us not to be afraid seem to imply that in this life, many things can make us feel afraid.

Of course there is paranoia and psychosis where people live with imaginary fears, or where fear can become pathological. But there are things and people to fear in this life!

Then there is a fear which serves as a caution in dangerous situations. Fear of falling and being killed keeps you from jumping out of an airplane without the help of a parachute.

And there is a fear which we are encouraged to have – the fear of the Lord – which we are told is the beginning of wisdom (Proverbs 9:10). We are admonished in Scripture to fear God and keep His commandments, for this is the whole duty of man (Ecclesiastes 12:13). The fear of God helps us to keep away from evil and obey God (Job 28:28).

But we can experience a debilitating fear when faced with adversity and when our survival appears to be threatened, for we no longer feel safe. In order for a person to feel safe, his most basic physiological needs for food, water, sleep, and more must be met. Anything that threatens our survival or safety can induce fear and worry.

That's why Matthew 6 is in the Bible. Jesus was giving a new twist to the reality of things. He was saying: *"I know these things are important for your survival in this life under the sun. I know that food and shelter are your basic needs and in order to survive, you must have these things. I know that you can be tempted to worry about these things that you need in your life. But your life is much more than that – and no matter how it looks to you, I will take care of you, just as I take care of the ravens, and the lilies, and the grass of the field. All these things are in my care..."*

*"Take no thought..."* *(Matthew 6:31).* Don't be overly worried. Don't be afraid. I will take care.

But we do become fearful. When bills mount up and we worry that we will lose our homes and we will be unable to take care of our families, when the very things we relied on for our sustenance and survival dry up, we get fearful.

I have struggled with fear for a lot of my life. When at around fourteen or fifteen, one of my young friends died from rheumatic fever, I was sure that I would be the next to die. I became a virtual hypochondriac!

I experienced fear again about two years later as I stood at the bed of a neighbor and family friend and watched as he wrestled with death from a massive heart attack.

When I went to university for the first time in 1968 I feared my mother would die while I was away studying. I used to worry about getting such a phone call. Years later, I stood at my mother's hospital bed and felt real fear as we watched death wrap its frigid hands around her body. The fear I felt was overwhelming.

Following her death, the grief and fear got all mixed up and felt the same to me. C.S. Lewis' description of the emotions he felt on the death of his wife, Joy, perfectly mirrors mine: "No one ever told me that grief felt so like fear. I am not afraid, but the sensation is like being afraid. The same fluttering in the stomach, the same restlessness, the yearning." [1]

Fear.

*"Elijah was a man of like passions as we are..." (James 5:17).* So do you think Elijah felt anxious as he saw his brook drying up? Do you think he panicked? Do you think he felt any fear at all? Or was he too spiritual and trusting for that?

Perhaps Elijah trusted God and was willing to wait and see just how God was going to take care of him. Maybe he did not have to wait long before God sent him on to His next plan of provision.

What about Abraham? Do you think Abraham felt any fear as he took his son to Mount Moriah to sacrifice him – His only son whom he loved – the son of promise, God's provision for seed more abundant than the sand of the sea and the stars of the heavens? Do you think he had anxious moments, even in his determination to obey God?

Were Elijah and Abraham superhuman? It is human to feel afraid, to wonder what's going to happen. How am I going to make it? God, are you really there? Life's experiences can indeed baffle us, stifle our faith, make us feel insecure, and fill us with fear, doubt, and worry.

But our God isn't insecure. He does not get so easily upset and befuddled by our floundering and our questions. He is not like us. His feelings are not so easily hurt.

*"He knoweth our frame, he remembereth that we are dust..."*
*(Psalm 103:14).*

*"Like as a father pitieth his children, so the Lord pitieth them that fear him" (Psalm 103:13).*

The following reminders and suggestions might help you just as they have helped me in dealing with fear:

*Remember – the spirit of fear is not from God.*

Fear can become a tyrannical master. It can paralyze us and prevent us from optimizing our abilities and potentialities. When fear takes control of our lives, it does not make us any less a Christian, or any less a child of God, but it can render ineffective the abundant life which Jesus Christ came to earth to give to all of His children who believe on His name (John 10:10).

God sent His Son, Jesus Christ, into this world to deliver His people from fear. Hebrews 2:9-18 confirms that Jesus was a partaker of flesh and blood so that through death He might destroy him that had the power of death, the devil, and deliver those who due to fear of death were subject to bondage throughout their lifetime.

It is not God's desire for His children to be bound by fear, lust, doubt, guilt, despair, panic, anger, or the like. Timothy, shy, fearful, and reticent, in danger of neglecting the gift that God had given him, was reminded by Paul that God has not given us a spirit of fear but a spirit of power and of love and of a sound mind (2 Timothy1:7).

*Remember – your struggle with fear does not preclude God using you.*

Timothy was the repository of the gift of God even though he was retiring and bashful by nature. So should you find that you are struggling with fear, overwhelmed, and intimidated by life, do not deride or belittle yourself. Amazingly, God often chooses *"the weak things of the world to confound the things which are mighty" (1 Corinthians 1:27b)*. It is truly all about God.

We do not know what Paul's "thorn in the flesh" was. Many have theorized about what it might have been, but that has been kept as one of the "secret things" that belong only to God. It serves to give encouragement to any of us in all our struggles – whatever they may be – that God's grace is indeed sufficient for us in all our weakness.

No astute modern-day Commander in Chief would have selected the Gideon we read about in Judges 6-8 to lead a military insurgency against the Midianites. But God selected him to deliver His people from the rule and oppression of the Midianites. Gideon was one fearful man, yet God called him a mighty man of valor!

God has not given us the spirit of fear, but God is the one who does the choosing and the using.

*Be careful – do not resign yourself to a life of fear.*

God can do anything. There is nothing that God cannot help us with or help us to overcome. In Genesis 18, God responded to Sarah's skeptical laugh when told she would conceive a child at age ninety with, *"Is anything too hard for the Lord?" (Genesis 18:14)*. In Numbers 11, Moses questioned how and where God could get flesh in the wilderness to feed the multitude of people and God told Moses, *"Is the Lord's hand waxed short?" (Numbers 11:23)*

In Luke 1, the angel Gabriel appeared to the Virgin Mary with the news that she was going to have a child – the Messiah, Jesus, the Christ. She did not understand how this could happen. Gabriel answered her, *"For with God nothing shall be impossible" (Luke 1:37)*.

God is able – abundantly able – to take away our fear.

*Acknowledge your fear.*

It is important to acknowledge your fear. Own up to it. Don't repress it. We often pretend we are not afraid when we are. We can become afraid of fear. We can be so plagued by this emotion that our response is to wear a mask. We become unable to acknowledge even to ourselves that we are afraid because of our fear.

One of the first steps we can take in overcoming the fear of fear is to acknowledge our fear and strip off the mask and pretense. Fear holds us hostage whenever we feel the need to pretend. It may sound simplistic, but I have discovered that whenever I tell my dentist, for example, that I feel anxious, my anxiety dissipates.

Trying to repress fear or push it down just won't work. The more we repress it the more it rears its head up and takes control of our lives.

It is a deep human need to make others feel that everything is okay. We are socialized to be overly concerned with what the significant and not-so-significant others in our lives think of us. We prefer to impress rather than to be real and true to ourselves. "Oh, don't worry about me. I'm fine. I'm too blessed to be stressed!" Good words. Are they true words?

*"He knoweth our frame. He remembereth that we are dust" (Psalm 103:14).*

*Let go of any embarrassment or hostility you may feel about your fear.*

We feel hostility and embarrassment because we are ashamed of our fear. We can be afraid of fear and also ashamed of fear. We believe and know that Christians should not be afraid – at least that's what we have been told. *"Why am I afraid?"* you ask yourself. You are embarrassed and dismayed by the fact that you are afraid. And you are angry that you are afraid and so embarrassed. You dare not let anyone know. Turmoil wells up in your spirit because you are so ashamed and embarrassed.

Let it go. Give the embarrassment and hostility to God.

*Refuse the guilt.*

Do not allow your life to be overrun by guilt because of those who may tell you that all these things are happening in your life, and you are feeling all of this fear because your faith is not big enough.

There are many indeed who struggle with faithless fear. Fear has eroded their faith. But adding guilt to this only compounds the problem. Jesus said all we need is faith as a grain of mustard seed – not a very big faith!

There are things that can happen in life that we should be afraid of. There is more to be afraid of than just fear itself. I would like to see any of us stand up in front of that 2004 tsunami in Indonesia and not run from it. Fear is what makes you run. Only a little child or an insane person would not run away from a tsunami out of fear, simply because they have no idea of the threat.

*There are threatening things in life.* We have to face threatening circumstances and threatening people sometimes. To acknowledge that and feel that does not mean we have no faith. We had better be afraid of some things and people, and get out of their way.

But in all of this Jesus' voice speaks to us, "Fear not..." He says this because He knows that as humans, we are inclined to fear people and circumstances. How many times do we see these words in the Bible? But God is with us and He has promised to take care of us. Fear not.

We need to hear Jesus' words so that fear does not paralyze us, deplete us, and make us unable to function. We need to hear Jesus' words so that fear does not erode our faith, because without faith it is impossible to please God. That can happen. It can happen to all kinds of people.

There are things to fear, but His gentle voice tells us:

*Trust me. Do not be afraid. I have everything in hand. Things are not out of control. I know your brook has become a trickle. I know the ravens have stopped coming. I know the brook has dried up. I know you are worried about how you are going to feed your children, send them to college, pay your mortgage, and pay your bills. I know that you feel as though you are on your own and you do not know what will happen in the future. Do not fear. I have it all in hand. Trust me.*

Don't allow any human person to make you live in guilt. Look to God.

*Share your feelings with someone you can trust.*

Find a trusted friend with whom you can share what you are going through. Not someone who will put you down, rush to advise you, or tell you how surprised they are that you feel that way. Find a person – preferably a Christian – who is able to listen to you, is trustworthy, and who will keep the matter confidential. They should understand the Scriptures, see life from a biblical perspective, and be someone with whom you can be accountable.

Psychotherapy and the Christian religion agree on the effectiveness of being able to share our "faults" with others. *"Confess your faults one to another* and pray for one another that *ye may be healed…" (James 5:16).* This is not validation or endorsement of setting up hierarchical relationships where the "superior" person grants absolution or pardon to the other. Rather, it attests to the efficacy of a relationship where openness, accountability, genuineness, mutual trust, and commitment to intercessory prayer are among the core conditions, and can lead to wholeness and healing.

*Remind yourself and God of what His Word says, of His promises to you.*

Reading and memorization of Scripture should be a preventative measure for all Christians. The psalmist says in Psalm 119:11, *"Thy word have I hid in my heart that I might not sin against thee."* When Jesus was tempted in the desert, He did not run to get Scripture and try to memorize it then. *He already had it hidden in His heart.*

We need to prepare for the onslaughts and attacks from the evil one, and from the world around us. We shouldn't just run to the Word when we are in a state of fear and panic, and things are not working for us. We need to hide the Word in our heart. Let this be the norm for our life. During times of panic, remind yourself and your Heavenly Father of what His Word says.

- Remind yourself that the Scriptures say that God has placed His Word above His name (Psalm 138:2b). This makes God's Word immutable. It cannot be changed, for it is impossible for God to lie (Hebrews 6:18). Remind yourself that God watches over His Word to fulfill it and to see that it is fulfilled (Jeremiah 1:12). Remind yourself that the eyes of the Lord are upon the righteous, and His ears are open unto their cry (Psalm 34:15, 1 Peter 3:12).

- Remind yourself that the eyes of the Lord run to and fro throughout the whole earth to show Himself strong on the behalf of those whose hearts are perfect toward Him (2 Chronicles 16:9).
- Remind yourself that though you are not perfect, through Jesus' death on the cross you have been accepted by the beloved (Ephesians 1:6).
- Remind God that He has promised to keep him in perfect peace whose mind is stayed on Him (Isaiah 26:3).
- Remind yourself that His Word tells us not to worry about anything but to pray about everything, which includes our fear, our doubt, our anxiety, our worry, our panic, our disappointments, our todays, our yesterdays, our tomorrows, and our dried-up brooks.

*"Be careful for nothing but in everything by prayer and supplication with thanksgiving let your requests be made known unto God" (Philippians 4:7).*

- Remind yourself and God that He has promised to take care of you. Remind Him every day and in every circumstance – when things are going well, and when things are not going well.
- Remind God of His promises when you awake and before you fall asleep at night. When you have no money in your pocket and when you have lots of money. Speak of His promises just as much as when you are looking for a job or when you've got the job you wanted.
- Let God know that you are standing on His Word when everything seems to be going your way and when it looks as if nothing is going your way. Let Him know that you will cling to His promises when it seems as if God has forgotten you and when no water is in the brook and the ravens have stopped coming.

- Remind God that your only help is from Him when you are sitting up and when you are lying down, or when you are walking about doing your chores and normal business.

*"I'm your child and you have promised to take care of me, and I trust in your Word because your Word is unchangeable. You cannot lie."*

It is not that God needs reminding. He is not a forgetful Father who takes lightly His promises to His children. It is an obligation He has taken upon Himself, and His obligations are not frightening or onerous to Him. Neither are they overwhelming or overbearing. They are not beyond Him nor do they stretch Him to any limit. But as we remind Him of His words to us, our faith and confidence in Him will grow. Faith comes as we hear the Word of God (Romans 10:17).

*Remember, His grace has no measure.*

And even though you may not have used this "preventative" measure of meditating on God's Word and hiding it in your heart, God's grace and mercy are such that you are still welcome to run to the Word and find "care and comfort and healing grace, hope for tomorrow and help for today." [2] In Psalm 119:92, the psalmist asserts, *"Unless thy law had been my delights, I should then have perished in mine affliction."*

There is absolutely no need to perish in our affliction. We can run to the Word. God's Word is living and powerful. Fill your mind with it. It is sharper than a two-edged sword. It is able to judge the thoughts and intents of the heart. It is a healing Word, a delivering Word, a sanctifying Word, a comforting Word. It is life and light, health, and wholeness.

Start your own "promises" journal. Write in it every day. Read it every day. God's Word will remove your fear. Believe me – it will.

*Pray – and don't stop praying.*

Prayer works. It does not matter what the world says. We may not understand how, but prayer works. *"The effectual fervent prayer of a righteous man availeth much" (James 5:16).* Keep in touch with your Heavenly

Father. Tell Him all about your fears, your doubts, your anxiety, and your disappointments. He is not angry with you because you are afraid. He is not upset because you feel fearful and doubtful and disappointed.

Do not estrange yourself from Him. Tell Him exactly what you are feeling, how you are feeling, and how afraid you are. Tell Him how embarrassed you are by your fear, how debilitating it is, and how it is paralyzing your life. Pray until the light breaks through – no matter how long that takes. And always remember faith is the antidote to fear.

*"You only need faith as the grain of a mustard seed..." (Matthew 17:20).*

Mustard seeds are the small seeds of the various mustard plants and are only 2mm in diameter. It is not the size of our faith, it is who we put our faith in that matters.

The Bible tells us in Romans 4:20 that Abraham *"staggered not at the promises of God."* I love the imagery here. He was strong in faith, being fully persuaded that what God had promised He could perform. But did Abraham show signs of anxiety? Did he question God's timing? Read the account in Genesis 22:1-19. How did he feel when time was passing and he and Sarah had no child? How did he feel taking Isaac to sacrifice him on Mount Moriah? He was persuaded that just as he was given Isaac "from the dead" – that is, his dead loins and Sarah's dead womb – God would in His way raise the young man back to life.

God hears our prayers – even our anxious prayers. In 1982, I was scheduled to have surgery in the UK. Understandably, our family was worried as this was only two years after my mother had died after not recovering from surgery. Two days prior to surgery, a terrifying and frightening fear invaded my body. It felt like something physical – like a huge knot in my chest. It was burdening me and weighing me down, but I told no one about it. My chest felt so tight and knotted up that I found myself unable to kneel and pray. But I lifted up my eyes to God in desperation. I made no audible prayers. I did not want to go into surgery filled with such fear.

I attended church on Sunday morning, the day before I was due to go into the hospital. The church organist, knowing I was scheduled for surgery, selected wonderful hymns of encouragement and trust in God. Usually I find hymns of the faith most encouraging and uplifting, but this time they did nothing to help me. I continued to feel burdened throughout the service, and throughout the time of prayer. I had certainly thought that I would be helped during prayer time or in the singing of the worship hymns. Nothing was helping. I waited for the sermon, hoping that God's Word would lighten my load.

The pastor spoke from Job 28:28. He spoke about the fear of the Lord. As he spoke, my heart sank further. He spoke about the fear of the Lord – what it means. At another time, I would have been challenged by this sermon, but I just could not get past this lump, this knot in my chest. I began to despair because it seemed that the sermon was coming to a close. No help for me today… or so I thought.

Just when I believed he was going to end the sermon, the pastor began to say that he wanted to talk about another kind of fear – a fear that God did not want us to have. He spoke of a fear that was superstitious and afraid that fed on foreboding, premonitions, and signs. He said that God told him to tell His people that He did not want us to have that fear. I listened, entranced. He was speaking to me, personally. *I knew this was God.* If I live to be one hundred years old, I could be awakened at midnight and be able to recall and relate what happened at this point in the service. As the pastor continued to speak, I felt the knot in my chest dissolve – miraculously, as if someone reached inside my chest and removed it – completely. It did not evaporate slowly. It just went away! All at once, the fear vanished.

I entered the hospital the next day full of confidence, trust, and hope in God.

So don't ever give up! Don't settle for less than what God promises you. God hears anxious prayers. He sends His word and heals us (Psalm 107:20).

Our great High Priest, Jesus, is touched with the feeling of our infirmity – whatever that infirmity might be.

He does not separate Himself from us because we are fearful, but comes ever closer.

He is Immanuel, God with us. God can use us in spite of our fear – just as He used Gideon! And He *can* and He *will* take away our fear.

> Thou art coming to a King,
> Large petitions with thee bring;
> For His grace and power are such,
> None can ever ask too much. [3]

## God is Sovereign in All His Works

We are all prone to make assumptions about what God may or may not do, sometimes based on our own personal schemas – preconceived ideas or mental structures which shape our understanding of who God is. But God does not always fit into our schemata of things, for He is sovereign and above all. He is therefore under no obligation to give us explanations about His determinations and provisions for our lives.

There are things that are secret – the understanding of them will always elude us. Deuteronomy 29:29 speaks about this: *"The secret things belong unto our God: but those things which are revealed belong unto us and to our children forever ."* We can ask as many "whys" as we want to, engage in as many philosophical debates and arguments as possible, but there will always remain those things that are secret – things we cannot comprehend or fathom.

Just because God deals one way with one person does not mean that He will deal with another in the same manner. He may use miraculous means to deliver and protect us or He may use ordinary natural means, or He may not "deliver" in the way we expect.

Elijah was told to hide. David had to run for his life from Saul. Joseph was warned in a dream to run to Egypt with Mary and the young child, Jesus. An angelic and heavenly army was dispatched to deliver Elisha and his servant from the army of the king of Samaria. The angel of God came to Peter's rescue. But James was beheaded. Stephen was stoned to death. *"And others were tortured, not accepting deliverance; that they may obtain a better resurrection" (Hebrews 11:35).*

I was sixteen or seventeen years old when I learned that we cannot presume or predict what God would or would not do, based on our finite understanding of Him. A prominent member of our church, a husband and father of several children, his family's primary provider, became ill. When he got ill, I assumed it would be a matter of time before he got better. *"God would never, ever let this man die,"* so I thought. But he died.

You might have had a similar experience where you felt absolutely certain that God would respond in a particular way. Like Namaan you might have said, *"Behold, I thought..." (2 Kings 5:11).*

Our finite minds cannot always predict the workings of God or what God will do. His designs may not make much sense to us, but He asks us to trust Him – His ways are higher than ours. God acts in accordance with His character, with who He is – omniscient, all-powerful, just, and righteous in all His ways, loving, forgiving, holy, kind, and compassionate. He is a God who does all things well.

He is sovereign in who and what He uses and chooses. An unclean raven to feed a Jewish prophet, a pagan prostitute to assist His people in Jericho… God is sovereign. He knows what He is about.

## We Must not Despise God's Means of Provision – Ever.

Why did God choose ravens to feed Elijah? In 2 Kings 5, Namaan, captain of the Syrian army, went to the prophet Elisha to be healed of leprosy. Elisha sent a messenger to Namaan and told him to dip seven times in the river Jordan in order to be healed of the disease. Namaan was very angry because he thought that the prophet would have come out to him, called on the name of his God, and laid hands on him. Additionally, he insisted, there were cleaner rivers in Damascus, better than all the waters of Israel, better than Jordan. *"May I not wash in them and be clean?" (2 Kings 5:12).* He had had his own thoughts about how things would and should be done.

Namaan despised the provision of healing that was being offered to him. He wanted to be healed, but he had his preconceived thoughts about *how* this healing would be provided. The Bible account tells us that he turned and went away in a rage (2 Kings 5:12). But his healing and deliverance lay in his obedience and trust in the word of the prophet. There was no more power in the river Jordan than any other river, but the power was in God's Word and its realization in his trusting and obeying His Word.

Namaan's servants were bold enough to challenge his pride and haughty attitude, and he had his flesh become again like the flesh of a little child, and he was made clean (2 Kings 5:14) as he humbled himself and accepted God's provision of healing.

So often we are prone to question. *Why does it have to be this way? Why does God have to use this person? Why couldn't God have chosen someone else, or something else? Why doesn't He do it the way I want Him to? Why doesn't He give me this job instead of that one?* We are in turmoil because the provision is not gift wrapped and tied with beautiful yellow or blue ribbons as we want or expected it to be. In fact, it really is a far cry from anything we would have expected God to do for us in our circumstance. So we question and complain and register our preferences and our dislikes.

One of the men who shared his testimony for this book observed that during the period of his dried-up brook, help would come from various sources. His mother and his wife's father were the main sources of help. But he said, "I felt guilty taking from them and my pride would force me to refuse it, but in essence I needed their help."

The children of Israel got into serious trouble with God for despising His means of provision. They needed to be nourished and fed in the wilderness, so God supplied them with manna. In Numbers 11 we see them complaining and griping. Surly and ungrateful, they reminisced with relish about the fish, the cucumbers, the melons, the leeks, and the onions they ate when they were slaves in Egypt – slaves in cruel bondage to the Egyptians! They lusted after and longed for their past experience as slaves to cruel and hateful masters.

*"But now our souls are dried away: there is nothing at all, beside this manna, before our eyes" (Numbers 11:6).*

God's wonderful, divine, supernatural provision became nothing in their eyes – something to be despised! They suffered as a result of this, for God smote the people with a very great plague, but even worse, he sent leanness in their soul (Psalm 106:15).

Aren't we much like the Israelites, oftentimes? We ask God for His help, but we don't like the way the help is provided or who He uses to provide the help. So we murmur and complain. First Corinthians 10:1-11 offers a stern warning against this type of attitude.

God has promised to provide grace, mercy, protection, peace, healing, His unfailing presence and all that we need that pertain to life and godliness.

Do we despise His means of provision? *That's too dirty... that's unclean... I won't touch that with a ten-foot pole... Oh no, folks like that – they're not my type... Oh, that's just a waste of my time.*

Are we willing to accept His means of provision? An unclean raven, a prostitute, a dirty river, a wasted day?

*"The judgments of the Lord are true and righteous altogether" (Psalm 19:9).*

71

## We Must Learn to Recognize God's Voice and Discern His Workings

Jeremiah 17:6 speaks of the man who trusts in man and in the arm of flesh. This is a person who is unable to see when good comes. The Scripture says that this man will inhabit the parched places of the wilderness in a salt land.

An important lesson from Cherith is that we have to be able to hear God's voice and discern His leading – no matter how strange or unexpected the leadings might appear. God told the prophet to go to Cherith. God told the prophet that he would be sustained at Cherith by ravens bringing bread and flesh. Elijah had to be able to hear God's voice and discern His directions and leading. And herein lies one of the greatest dilemmas of the modern-day Christian: How do we differentiate the voice of our own desires and wishes as opposed to the voice of God speaking to us – especially if our wishes are legitimate, "spiritual," and seem as if they portend good and not evil?

This is the dilemma of the present-day believer because God no longer speaks audibly to us as it would appear that He did to some of His followers in earlier eras, especially in Old Testament times.

Moses is described as a man with whom God spoke *"face to face" (Exodus 33:11).* Abraham and the patriarchs – Samuel, Ezekiel, Jeremiah, and Hosea – heard God's audible voice speak His directions and directives to them. Paul, then Saul, was apprehended by God on the way to Damascus and heard a voice speak to him. Those who accompanied him heard the sound even though they were unable to decipher the words.

But Hebrews 1 tells us, quite emphatically, that *"God, who at sundry times and in divers manners spake in time past unto the fathers by the prophets, hath in these last days spoken to us by His Son" (Hebrews 1:1).*

This does not mean that we can place God in a box. None of us can emphatically say what God will or will not do – except keep His word, be just and holy in all His ways, and not lie. But in His actual dealings with His children – He is sovereign.

My mother spoke to us often of the time when both her and her sister planned to leave Montserrat to go to live in Trinidad with one of their aunts who was the pastor of a small Pentecostal church. Sadly, the man who had promised to loan her the fare was unable to provide the funds on time and her sister, who already had her fare, tearfully went on ahead with my mother promising that she would be on the very next boat.

Before she could leave, one night she dreamed that a lady approached her and told her that she wouldn't be going to Trinidad because she was going to be a worker right in Montserrat. She woke up from the dream perturbed and worried. It had seemed so real. She spoke to several older and wiser believers, many of whom comforted her spirit by telling her it was just a dream. After all, she was going to be with her relatives and her aunt was a preacher. She recalled that only one person cautioned her about paying some attention to the dream. She did not want to. She wanted to be with her sister in Trinidad. They were very close.

She continued with her plans to leave, but another night she had a dream and this time she was directed to a passage in the Bible. When she awoke, she found the scripture passage in Job 33:14-15: *"For God speaketh once, yea twice, yet man perceiveth it not. In a dream, in a vision of the night, when deep sleep falleth upon men, in slumbering upon the bed."*

My mother remained in Montserrat and God used her in a mighty way as a worker in the Pentecostal churches there, alongside my Dad.

My mother had heard from God just as Elijah, Moses, Paul, and Peter had.

So how then do we learn to hear from God? I am certainly not advocating relying on dreams as a means of hearing and understanding the voice of God. The point I am making is that God is sovereign in all His works and in all His dealings with His children.

But the answer can and only will be the same for us as for the patriarchs and prophets with whom God spoke face to face.

We have to draw nigh to Him and He will draw nigh to us (James 4: 8).

We have to be those who read, study, meditate upon, and obey the Scriptures. We have to hide these words in our heart. We have to have a consistent personal and private relationship with the Lord. We have to let Him know that "we can't even walk without Him holding our hands," [4] and He will let His Word become a lamp unto our feet and a light unto our path. It will guide us in the darkest of night and on the loneliest of trails.

There is no intention ever on God's part to confuse His children or to have them walk in the dark. His Word is light and life. He led His children in the wilderness with a pillar of cloud by day and a pillar of fire by night and never took them away until they reached the Promised Land. In the same manner, His Word will direct our paths, give us clarity and clarification, and make our paths of duty straight and plain before our face until we get to Heaven.

But does this mean we will never ever again misunderstand God's leading and make a wrong decision? Of course not.

We are not divine. We are human. We are, as G. Rawson, the writer of the beautiful hymn "O Worship the King" says, "Frail children of dust and feeble as frail." [5] We may yet flounder and misunderstand God's direction, but when that happens, hopefully it will not have been done out of rebellion, disobedience, and self-seeking. And even when it is and we ask forgiveness, grace steps in and our God works all things together for our good and for His glory.

Isaiah 50:10-11 sheds some light here. This verse has been like a glowing and shining ray of light to me, an anchor for my soul during periods of darkness when I did not what to do: *"Who is among you that feareth the Lord, that obeyeth the voice of his servant, that walketh in darkness, and hath no light? Let him trust in the name of the Lord and stay upon his God."*

When we don't quite know what God is saying or where He is leading us, it is not the time to *"kindle our own fires and compass ourselves in sparks" (Isaiah 50:11).* It is not the time to walk in the light of the fire and sparks we have kindled. In other words, it is not the time to rely on our own wisdom, knowledge, ability, or skills in order to find our way and forge our own paths.

No. *It is the time to trust in the name of the Lord and rest upon God.*

As we wait on Him, as we wait for Him, as we rest in Him, He will make the path of duty straight and plain before our face.

## There is Interconnectedness between Life Experiences and Spiritual Dryness.

Spiritual dryness and many life experiences are often interconnected. Ahab married a pagan woman. First Kings 16:29-34 gives us some history. She was a Baal worshipper and Ahab too worshipped Baal, as did many other of the people of Israel – God's chosen people. This provoked God to anger. The following three and a half years of drought in the land epitomized the spiritual drought that ravaged the land of Israel because of Ahab's actions.

David's wandering in the dessert, as he ran away from Saul, kept him away from the sanctuary and other celebrants of worship, and this resulted in his experiencing spiritual dryness and barrenness in his life. And we have already spoken at some length about Job's wife. Her life experiences became a calamity too great for her to bear – they plunged her into spiritual dryness and drought. She lost her faith, she could no longer believe in a good God, or perhaps even a God at all for that matter. In her mind, death had to be better than to live with this existential angst, this worry about an unreliable God. She became a spiritual casualty along the way of life.

*"Curse God and die…" (Job 2:9).*

In Revelation 3:14-19, the church of the Laodiceans had grown rich and as a result self-satisfied. Because they had increased in material wealth and possessions, they began to feel that they had need of nothing – certainly not a close walk with God. Their wealth and increase made them feel secure, rich and among the best of the best.

In a startling letter to the leader of this church, God reveals how dried up and deficient they really were. His assessment is as biting as it is penetrating. They did not know, He said, that they were wretched and miserable, and poor, and blind, and naked.

> *"I counsel thee to buy of me gold tried in the fire, that thou mayest be rich; and white raiment, that thou mayest be clothed, and that the shame of thy nakedness do not appear; and anoint thine eyes with eye-salve, that thou mayest see" (Revelation 3:18).*

Life experiences can affect our spiritual condition – our walk with God. I read the book by Elie Wiesel, *Night*, two or three years ago. I read it again quite recently. The unimaginable suffering the author witnessed and experienced at the Auschwitz concentration camp, and then at Buchenwald eroded the religious zeal which he had as a thirteen-year-old boy. On Yom Kippur, as a prisoner, he refused to fast as some of the other prisoners suggested they should. "As I swallowed my ration of soup, I turned that act into a symbol of rebellion, of protest against Him." [6]

In the face of baffling and overwhelming life experiences, some lose their faith and trust in God. They dry up spiritually. They feel empty, bereft, with nothing left – no trust, no faith, no confidence, no hope.

For others, material prosperity, wealth, fame, and abundance make them self-reliant and self-satisfied, and they begin to trust more in themselves and fail to trust in God. The result is the same: spiritual dryness.

But your life experiences can draw you to God, for the antidote to spiritual dryness is just that – trust, faith, hope in, and complete reliance on the living God.

# Chapter 5

## Zarephath – More than Enough

❦

*"Arise, get thee to Zarephath..."*
*1 Kings 17:9*

She is afraid. She is very afraid. All that is left in her house to eat is a handful of meal with a little oil in a jug to bake a cake for her and her son. She has no one to whom she can turn for help, for everyone in her city is suffering because of the drought.

In her thirty plus years, she thinks, she has never, never experienced such a terrible drought.

She and her son had not yet succumbed to the drought only because of her prudence and frugality. Since her husband had died many years before, she had to learn how to be frugal, how to save and put aside something "for a rainy day" – or this time, a day without rain.

But now everything is gone. The drought has devoured everything. The animals perished and all the crops scorched and dried up.

She knows that she and her son will die. She wishes she could do something, but she is helpless. She thinks about her son. She loves him so much. He is her only reminder of her dear husband.

She goes outside and looks around at the parched fields surrounding her house. As far as her eyes see everything is dry and brown and barren. Like a wilderness.

"How I wish a miracle could happen to save him," she says to herself.

She goes to the back of her house to gather some sticks to make the fire for their meal. Their last meal. She is so afraid. And then she hears a voice, someone calling out to her. She turns around, startled. She had not seen anyone approaching.

It's an older man. She looks at him and gasps, for she recognizes him immediately. Elijah. That prophet from Israel. She had heard that he was the one who brought on the drought. King Ahab had sent around everywhere looking for him, and some men had passed by looking for him, giving her his description.

She has never seen him before, but everyone in the city of Zarephath has heard about him because he stood up to the wicked queen Jezebel. Not even her father, King Ethbaal, was able to stand up to Jezebel, a wicked, evil woman. But this man had. She had always wanted to see him or meet him. She believed in his God.

"Bring me a little water," he says. "I am very thirsty."

*"That's the least I can do for a man who has stood up to this terrible woman,"* she says to herself.

She turns to go inside for water.

"Bring me something to eat too. A piece of bread. I have not eaten for several days and I'm hungry." She stops and turns around.

"Believe me, I'm sorry. But I swear to you on the name of your God, I don't have anything left to give you. All I have is a handful of meal and a little oil. I just came outside to get some sticks to prepare a meal for me and my son. It will be our very last meal. After that, we will just wait to die."

"Don't be afraid," he says. "Do just what you have said you are going to do, but make a cake for me first. Bring it to me and afterward, prepare the rest for you and your son. I promise you, in the name of the Lord God of Israel, you will find that there's always meal in your barrel and oil in your jug until the rains come again."

She finds herself obeying the prophet without questioning. She empties the meal into a bowl and makes a cake for him with the oil that she has left. She takes it outside to him with the water.

She goes back inside and looks in the barrel. Her heart lurches, almost jumps out of her chest. There is meal in the barrel. She glances across and sees that the oil cruse is full.

*A miracle.*

*"And the barrel of meal wasted not, neither did the cruse of oil fail according to the word of the Lord, which He spake by Elijah" (1 Kings 17:16).*

There is meal and oil, day in and day out, night and day… every day. Enough for her, her son, and Elijah until the rains begin to fall again.

## MORE THAN ENOUGH?

The point of this book has been to ask the question, "Is God more than enough when our resources diminish? Is He enough when all the things we have relied on for sustenance evaporate and disappear – health, relationships, livelihood, employment, finances?"

How in all practicality is God more than enough when He does not answer or does not appear to answer, when a person feels let down, misled, disappointed, or even mistreated by God?

A book which had a tremendous impact on me shortly after my mother's death was Rabbi Harold Kushner's work, *When Bad Things Happen to Good People*. In it, he writes:

"The misfortunes of good people are not only a problem to the people who suffer and to their families. They are a problem to everyone who wants to believe in a just and fair and livable world. They inevitably raise questions about the goodness, the kindness, even the existence of God…" [1]

Is it that God is willing to help but unable to, or able to help but unwilling? Does God go to sleep? Does He forget about any of His children? Can things get out of control for Him?

Is life unfair? Does God give us more than we can bear? Is it really true that when we come to the end of all that we have and have held dear, and are left only with God, we would find that He is more than enough?

How can we be instructed in our questions by this account in 1 Kings 18?

## DRIED-UP BROOKS HAPPEN

For Elijah, his brook was the waters at the river Cherith, God's place of promised provision.

For the men whose stories I told in this book, their brooks were secure employment and the ability to take care of their family as they would like to. For others, the brook was good health or cherished, loving relationships.

For the widow from Zarapheth, her brook was the barrel of meal and the jug of oil. Because of the drought she had just enough left for a final meal which she was preparing for her and her son.

Her hope too had dried up and fled. *"I am gathering two sticks, that I may go in and dress [the meal] for me and my son that we may eat it, and die" (1 Kings 17:12).*

Dried-up brooks happen because we are living in a fallen world where bad things just happen. Relationships get sour and break up. Finances deplete. People lose their jobs and once healthy people get very ill. We age and lose strength and ability, and our sense of usefulness and prominence.

Or sometimes the savor and zest for life just dries up because we are tired, overwhelmed, and overstressed – even though it may appear to others as if we have it all as far as success and earthly possessions go.

We lose all our life savings and are left with nothing.

Calamitous and devastating things happen. We've witnessed this in Haiti, in New Orleans, in Mississippi, and in the island of Montserrat. Parents who have lost a child have had front row seats at such events and experiences.

Born into this world, we become subject to the sufferings and afflictions that are all part of life. Job 14:1 puts it succinctly, *"Man that is born of a woman is of few days, and full of trouble."* The only escape is never to have been born or to die. Job alludes to this in Job 3:9-12. Listen to his plaintive laments: *Why was I ever born? Why was I not stillborn? Why wasn't my mother barren?*

He recognizes that this is *life*.

Dried-up brooks also happen as a consequence of our own actions – because of our backsliding and disobedience, and can represent a form of God's chastening. If our dried-up brooks happen because God is chastening us, His ultimate goal is our good – our best good.

The Bible is clear. When we are judged by God and chastened by Him, this ensures that we escape the final judgment with the rest of the world. Even in His chastening of His children God is looking out for us. In 1 Corinthians 11:32 we find encouragement: *"But when we are judged, we are chastened of the Lord, that we should not be condemned with the world."*

Hebrews 12 is encouraging and reassuring. It admonishes us not to despise the chastening hand of God. *"For whom the Lord loveth he chasteneth and scourgeth every son whom he receiveth" (Hebrews 12:6).* It is precisely because God loves us as His sons and daughters that He chastens us, and even though while it is continuing it is not a joyous but rather a grievous experience, yet *"... afterward it yieldeth the peaceable fruit of righteousness unto them which are exercised thereby" (Hebrews 12:11).*

God is always looking out for our best good – even when we are being chastened by Him.

Dried-up brooks happen because we are being tried and tested. In the end we will come forth as pure gold. This is not chastening. This is testing. Our faith is being tried. It can be a perplexing experience because most often we do not and cannot understand what is happening in our lives. It is perplexing because it may be prolonged and it can seem as if the difficulties and hardship will never end.

We may examine ourselves and confess our sins, yet the situation in our lives may continue unabated. We really do not know how much time passed between I Kings 17:7 and 1 Kings 17:8. Neither do we know how long Job had to wait before God revealed Himself to him and restored all that he had and more.

Abraham waited twenty-five years until both he and Sarah were old and stricken in years. Joseph waited seventeen years before God's purpose for him was eventually fulfilled. They were being tried and tested.

Our trial of our faith in God, according to 1 Peter 1:7, is much more precious than gold which is tried. God is an active participant in the trial and testing of the believer. Malachi pictures Him sitting with His children throughout the entire process – just like what a refiner and purifier of silver does (Malachi 3:2-3). He never leaves our side, carefully watching over us, regulating, never taking His eyes off His children.

One day, He will purge us as gold and silver, and our lives will become an offering of righteousness unto our God.

There will indeed be an afterward.

Dried-up brooks happen for the express purpose of turning the hearts of God's people back to Him – away from earthly trusts, away from self-reliance, away from activities and earthly endeavors, away from relying on our personal agendas and schemes of thinking – back to the living God.

The children of Israel did not totally forsake worship of Jehovah. They incorporated Baal worship into their worship of God. They had their own idea of worship. Elijah, zealous for God, became angry and prayed for God to send famine. He wanted the people to understand once and for all that there was only one true God. He sent rain. He could stop the rain.

God answered the prophet's prayer and stopped the rain from falling for three and a half years so that the people would understand that the Lord is God, and return to Him.

Dried-up brooks happen in the believer's life. God allows these or sends them for the best good of His own.

## DRIED-UP BROOKS CAN SEEM MORE MENACING WHEN GOD SEEMS NOT TO BE PAYING ATTENTION

Not all of us have been able to "name it and claim it." Many, many of God's children have had their brooks dry up and have had to cry out like the psalmist David in Psalm 13:1-2: *"How long will thou forget me, O Lord? Forever? How long wilt thou hide thy face from me? How long shall I take counsel in my soul, having sorrow in my heart daily? How long shall mine enemy be exalted over me?"*

God can allow afflictions and difficulties to reach extremities and limits beyond our natural endurance – no matter how much we beg and plead.

For every Psalm that praises God for His mercies and goodness, there is one in which the psalmist cries out to God in desperation, begging and beseeching Him to arise, wake up, look upon his condition – to do something.

Look at this complaint (Psalm 10:1): *"Why standest thou afar off, O Lord? Why hidest thou thyself in times of trouble?"* And this one, *"Arise, O Lord; lift up thine hand: forget not the humble"* (Psalm 10:12).

In Psalm 44:13-26, the psalmist describes the troubles and adversities God's children have been experiencing. They have become a reproach, a byword, a shaking of the head among the ungodly. In verse 23 he implores God: *"Awake, why sleepest thou, O Lord? Arise, cast us not off forever."*

Asaph had experienced troubles in his life to the point where he began to feel that he had served God in vain. Those who were wicked and ungodly seemed to be prospering. They had no problems, did not lose their jobs, did not face foreclosure on their homes, but he who had *"cleansed his heart and washed his hands in innocency"* (Psalm 73:13) found himself plagued with problems and difficulties day in and day out. *Morning was not a blessing, but a terrifying thought.*

Many have come to the point of almost losing their faith because they come to God and find what seems to be a closed door. Not even a movement of a curtain at a window. Nothing. Those who experience dried-up brooks have found this to be the most trying of all – God's seeming silence. It is as if He is not paying attention, not listening to their prayers and cries. It is perplexing when prayer becomes a one-sided affair.

I believe Joseph felt like that in prison. After all, he had done nothing wrong. He was imprisoned for doing the moral and right thing! Surely it would not be long before God would come through for him. The incident with the king's butcher and baker must have perked up his spirits. Surely it made him feel this was surely the harbinger of good things – his vindication, his release, what he desired most.

Has that ever happened to you? Have you ever endured a particular trial and then something ensued which made you feel sure, very sure that your time had come – your time of deliverance. Things were going to change from then on. This is my moment! you thought.

In his eagerness and impatience, Joseph told the chief butler not to forget him and to make mention of him to Pharaoh. Joseph must have waited with baited breath every day for the call of his release to come. But the chief butler did not remember Joseph. He forgot him. Two full years passed and Joseph was still in prison. He must have felt as if someone was playing games with him!

Have you ever felt that way? Has this ever been your experience? You have travailed and interceded over some issue in your life, sought God's help, sought His divine intervention, searched for the sign of a cloud – it didn't even have to be bigger than the size of a man's fist – but it seems God is not paying any attention.

## GOD OFTEN GIVES US MORE THAN WE CAN BEAR

I know that it is commonly said and thought by many that God does not give us more than we can bear. How many times have you heard someone say that to another suffering believer? My husband has continued to refute this belief. He insists that God gives us or allows to come our way things that are *more than we can bear.* He argues that if God didn't, why would we need to call on Him? We would just simply work things out ourselves. We would not need to call on God for help. But our burdens are often so much heavier than we can bear, so we have to rely on Him. We have to call on His name.

The widow woman and her son in Zarephath faced a slow death from famine and hunger. The prospect of her son's death must have been unbearable for her to contemplate. She was absolutely powerless to help herself and her son.

Her response to Elijah's request for a cake is an almost stoic, resigned *"...I am gathering two sticks, that I may go and dress it for me and my son, that we may eat it and die" (1 Kings 17:12).* She had nothing left. There was no hope on the horizon, no prospects of any help. She had reached the end of her rope. She could turn to no one for help because everyone else was in the same boat. The suffering and despair was ubiquitous. Everyone was dying and waiting to die. It was more than she could bear.

On Sunday April 25, 2010, I watched the memorial service on television for the 29 miners who were killed in the explosion in West Virginia. I was particularly touched by the remarks made by Sen. Jay Rockefeller. Among the many things he said, he observed, "It is almost too much to bear."

There have been times when I have felt as if I had been given more than I could bear. One such time was when my father died. It was just a few weeks before my wedding when he became ill. In spite of much prayer, pleading, and supplication, he died. His funeral was exactly one week before my scheduled wedding date. But all I have gone through perhaps pales in comparison with what others have endured.

I have mentioned the book *Night* by Elie Wiesel. It is a heart wrenching account of what the Jewish people suffered at the hands of other human beings in concentration camps. The author tells of the rabbi who always prayed and was able to recite entire pages from the Talmud. But the suffering the rabbi experienced and saw at Auschwitz tore away at his belief and faith.

"It's over. God is no longer with us.... I suffer hell in my soul and my flesh. I also have eyes and I see what is being done here. Where is God's mercy? Where's God? How can I believe, how can anyone believe in this God of Mercy?" [2]

When we get more than we can bear, our heart and our flesh cry out.

The rabbi at Auschwitz was not alone in his despair. He might have remembered Asaph. In Psalm 73, Asaph found himself almost on the verge of hanging up his hat, throwing in the towel – giving up on God. *"But as for me, my feet were almost gone: my steps had well nigh slipped"* (Psalm 73:2). His distress and anguish were relentless:

> *"For all day long have I been plagued, and chastened every morning"* (Psalm 73:14).

> *"My flesh and my heart faileth . . ."* (Psalm 73:26).

Job too was completely baffled by his experience. He felt hedged in by God (Job 3:23), unable to plead his cause before God (Job 9:32-33), and unjustly treated (Job 17:11-17).

Lest we think that this happened only in the Old Testament under the old covenant, let us look at the Apostle Paul, who in 2 Corinthians 1:8, speaks of the troubles they faced in Asia. Look at the superlatives. They were pressed out of measure, above strength, insomuch that they *despaired even of life.* They thought they would die in the process. Whatever they faced felt like more than they were able to bear.

Into the lives of God's children come experiences that are far beyond our power to bear or negotiate. These experiences press us out of measure. They are above or more than our strength to the point where we may even despair of life.

How then do we bear what is impossible to bear?

## GOD HELPS US TO BEAR

The secret lies in the latter part of Psalm 73:26, and 2 Corinthians 1:9.

Asaph says, *"My flesh and my heart faileth but God is the strength of my heart and my portion forever,"* and the Apostle Paul notes, *"But we had the sentence of death in ourselves that we should not trust in ourselves but in God which raiseth the dead."*

The answer is God. That's how we bear. God. Who He is – not what He can give us. Not what He can bless us with. Not what He can do for us. But God Himself.

> We *bear* by running to – not running away from God.
> We bear by sitting at His feet and waiting upon and for Him.
> And what kind of God is He? What are His attributes?

Is He a God who plays games with His children – afflicting them for His own selfish purpose, just to watch them shiver and squirm?

Is He a master chess player, setting us up to bring us down, so that cringing and crying, we may run to Him?

Lamentations 3:33-35 offers some enlightenment: *"For [God] doth not afflict willingly nor grieve the children of men. To crush under His feet all the prisoners of the earth, To turn aside the right of a man before the face of the most high, To subvert a man in his cause, the Lord approveth not."*

God is not like some capricious mythological Greek god who enjoys seeing his subjects suffer. He does not play games with His children. He gets no perverse pleasure from seeing us squirm and panic in our frustration and pain. He says that not even in the death of the sinner does He derive any pleasure (Ezekiel 33:11).

And what does God say about Himself? He says He is a jealous God. No need to defend God here – He is jealous. No other God but me. Not negotiable. Exodus 20:5 states it explicitly, *"I the Lord am a jealous God."* He does not tolerate or condone idolatry. And what else does He say about Himself? He is merciful and gracious, longsuffering and abundant in goodness and truth, keeping mercy for thousands, and forgiving iniquity, transgression, and sin (Exodus 34:6-7).

Asaph, in all his despair and despondency, went to the house of God, listened to the Word of God, and found God to be the strength of his heart and his portion forever. His heart was failing but God revived, renewed, and refreshed him.

*"He leadeth me beside the still waters. He restoreth my soul"* *(Psalm 23:2).*

Asaph found God to be his portion. A Rock, a Shield, a Defender. A Provider, a Guide. Faithful. Just. Good – all he needed and more!

*"The Lord is my Shepherd I shall not want"* *(Psalm 23:1).*

Asaph found that this God was sufficient not just yesterday and today but forever.

His portion forever. Never failing, never-ending God. Always there.

*"Surely goodness and mercy shall follow me all the days of my life"*
*(Psalm 23:6).*

Asaph's brook of hope and trust may have just about dried up, but when he went into God's house and heard His Word, he understood who God was. He realized the ignorance and foolishness of his envy of the prosperity of the wicked. He experienced God. He renewed His relationship with Him. He felt the assurance of His presence:

*"Nevertheless I am continually with thee: thou hast holden me by my right hand" (Psalm 73:23).*

He became able to bear the injustices of life because he drew near to God and understood again who God was – his strength and all that he would ever need.

Whether life becomes more than we can bear because we live in such a fallen world, or because we are being chastened by our Heavenly Father, or because we are being tested and tried, or because He seeks to turn our hearts back to Him, we are able to bear what life brings because of God. Through God. With God.

He is the help and health of our countenance. He is our refuge and our strength.

So when life seems more than we can bear, the answer is God Himself.

Our family had a very dear friend who was like a sister to my siblings and I, and a daughter to my parents. She has now gone to be with the Lord. She seemed to have had more than her fair share of suffering. A few weeks before she died, her sister told me that any other person who had gone through what she had would have given up already, "But her faith in God is so strong."

She left the island of Montserrat at an early age to better her life and herself. She succeeded in doing that. She was successful in her chosen career. She qualified as a registered nurse, a real estate agent, and a human services counselor. She worked in pediatric, medical surgical care and psychiatric nursing. She became very active in her community and in her church. She never forgot her God. She loved the Lord and served Him diligently. She had come to know Him at an early age and continued to follow Him faithfully. But ill health set in. It began with a fall in 1992 from which she suffered a severe injury to her right knee. Eventually, because of various complications arising from a diabetic condition, she had to give up employment and retire early because of ill health. By age fifty-six she was almost completely disabled.

Various surgeries and health crises followed. There were times she reported that she almost did not make it, but God helped her through. A few years ago, while disabled, she fell and broke both her legs. Her stay in the hospital was long and arduous. The doctor was not sure then that she could survive one surgery, never mind two. The operations were performed two days apart. But she survived, much to the surprise of the medical staff. She lived to see another day and was able to return to her home.

A few months ago I called her on a Wednesday morning. Her sister answered the phone. She was in the hospital. She had had surgery on Monday. Following that surgery, the doctors realized there was another serious, life-threatening problem, so she had to be taken back into surgery again on Wednesday. At the time we were speaking, she was still in surgery.

We chatted after she got out of hospital. I had never heard her sound so tired and frail. She said that she had gone through a rough time, but God was good. I told her about my book and that I wanted to include her experience in it. I asked her how she made it. How did she *bear*? She told me, "You can't give up and you won't give up with a thankful heart. You are thankful – not for everything, but in everything."

And she was not pretending. You cannot pretend when your suffering is so great. I saw it in her life when we visited with her a few years ago. She found it possible to have joy in God.

The answer for her was God – trusting in Him, believing what He says, and resting on His promises.

She had found out the secret. She learned how to *bear* when life seemed more than she could bear.

## THIS GOD IS ALWAYS AT WORK ON BEHALF OF HIS CHILDREN

The ravens did not *decide* to bring bread and flesh to Elijah every day, morning, and evening. It was God who commanded the ravens to feed Elijah at Cherith, just as it was God who *commanded* the widow woman in Zarephath to feed Elijah. God was working behind the scenes to ensure the sustenance of the prophet Elijah.

But God also allowed Elijah's brook to dry up so that the widow herself could be provided for. The woman was a Gentile, but God miraculously provided for her just as He did for His prophet. Jesus alluded to this in the gospels. In His sovereign power and grace, God chose to provide sustenance for this widow and sent Elijah to her, even though there were many widows in Israel at the time. It was all God's doing.

God had planned and prepared beforehand for the sustenance of Elijah and that of the widow and her son. Elijah eventually realized that God had sent him to Zarapheth not just for his own sustenance but even more so for the sustenance of the widow woman and her son.

At times this is difficult to believe, to accept, because God seems to be standing far off from us. We cannot see how He is working and things seem to go from bad to worse. We look in the barrel and there is only a handful of meal left and just enough oil for one more meal. There is famine and drought in the land. All the brooks have dried up.

A song I heard for the first time in the 1980's, written by Bryan Jeffery Leech, expresses this thought so eloquently. Some of you reading may well remember it:

When God says "No" to you, it's such a blow to you
When all your hopes and dreams unravel at the seams
When God says "wait" to you, When God seems late to you
It's hard to rest beneath His will
It's hard to trust and just be still
It's hard to wait until it's simply all made plain.

Chorus:
He who holds us in His hands has no problems, only plans
He who has control of all sees the smallest sparrow fall
He who acts when no one knows
Does not sleep as we suppose
But works in all things, in great or small things
For His own glory and our best good.

When God works silently in ways we cannot see
When troubles multiply so that we ache and sigh
When God does not seem kind
When hope is hard to find

It's hard to rest within His will
It's hard to trust and just be still
It's hard to simply wait until it's all made plain. [3]

I had overextended myself financially when I built my house back in 1989. At the time, I needed to have the kitchen cupboards done, but I was short of money and found it very difficult to locate a carpenter who would do the work for me. Furthermore, it was just after Hurricane Hugo had devastated the island and most carpenters were busy replacing roofs on the many houses that had been destroyed by the hurricane. It was a very demoralizing and anxious time in my life. Many days I was so discouraged and wished I had never undertaken such a project.

Eventually a carpenter showed up. His wife had told him I needed a carpenter and he decided to help me. The arrangement was that he would do the work and be paid ten thousand dollars on completion. I did not know how I would pay him as I did not have the money, but I agreed. He did an excellent job. As the time approached when I knew I would have to come up with the payment, having no other recourse, I decided to sell my car. I spoke to a few people, but could find no one who was willing to pay me more than eight thousand dollars.

In hope of getting the car sold, I took it to the mechanic for a tune-up. On the afternoon I was to pick up the car, as we drove on to Church Road we saw an accident near the Texaco gas station. My sister said to me, "But Blondina, it looks like your car." My heart sank. How could it be? I needed to sell the car. But it was indeed my car. One of the young mechanics had taken the car without permission and crashed it.

The owners of the mechanic shop, who were also car dealers, were very apologetic and offered me a new car, less the amount the car was insured for, or a cash payment in the insured amount. Yes, the insured amount was ten thousand! Two weeks or so later, after my carpenter had pounded in the last nail and put the final touches on my beautiful kitchen cabinets, I joyfully and thankfully paid him the full amount. Ten thousand! This was nothing short of miraculous provision! God worked behind the scenes in a most unexpected and remarkable way. Hallelujah!

We learn from the account in 1Kings 17 that God is always at work – most often behind the scenes looking out for His children, working on their behalf. *"For the eyes of the Lord run to and fro throughout the whole earth to shew Himself strong in the behalf of those whose heart is perfect toward Him" (2 Chronicles 16:9).*

## WE MUST VENTURE WHOLLY ON THIS GOD. GOD DEMANDS THIS.

> *Venture on Him, venture wholly*
> *Let no other trust intrude.* [4]

God told Elijah to do a most unusual thing: go to a widow for help. Walvoord and Zuck note in *The Bible Knowledge Commentary* that widows were usually poor people who would normally run out of food first in a famine. Seeing that the famine was created by a drought, going to a widow for help was a strange directive. [5]

The very thing the widow needed in order to stay alive – food – God asked her to let go of. She had just enough for her final meal. The prophet told her, *"make me thereof a little cake first"* (1 Kings 17:13).

The rich young ruler was told, *"go and sell that thou hast and give to the poor... and come and follow me" (Matthew 19:21).*

Abraham's requirement was particularly heart wrenching. At least for the rich young ruler, it was only possessions he was being asked to give up. God said to Abraham, *"Take now thy son, thine only son Isaac, whom thou lovest, and get thee into the land of Moriah; and offer him there for a burnt offering upon one of the mountains" (Genesis 22:2).*

The story is told of a man who fell off a cliff. He hung on to some roots at the edge of the cliff but realized he would not be able to hold on too long. Beneath him was the precipice he would fall into if his hands slipped. He would never survive such a fall.

In despair he began to shout, "Help, somebody help me! God? Help me! Please!"

He immediately heard a reverberating voice above say, "Let go."

And just as quickly he responded, "Anybody else up there?"

This is a humorous anecdote which nevertheless teaches how difficult and indeed frightening it can sometimes be to venture on God since this may involve letting go of what we hold dear or what we believe may be vital to our very existence, security, well-being, and survival.

Venturing may mean letting go of people, things, assumptions, concepts, preconceived ideas, and agendas with which we have grown familiar and which we believe are indispensable to our personal happiness and growth. It can be a difficult and sometimes scary process when we do not *know* and understand God.

Venturing wholly on God means that He alone becomes our trust, hope, and confidence. We let go of all other trusts. God demands this.

In venturing wholly on God:

## WE MUST DRAW NEAR

It is in drawing near that we come to truly know and understand God. Even though we cannot understand everything about God, we can enter into a relationship with Him where we understand who He is, where He communicates with us personally through His Word and through the promptings of the Holy Spirit, and where we communicate with Him in prayer. Jeremiah 10:23-24 explains this amazing relationship:

> *Thus saith the Lord, Let not the wise man glory in his wisdom, neither let the mighty man glory in his might, let not the rich man glory in his riches. But let him that glorieth glory in this, that he understandeth and knoweth me, that I am the Lord which exercise loving-kindness, judgment, and righteousness in the earth: for in these things I delight, saith the Lord.*

The account in 1 Kings 17 states that God commanded the widow woman to feed Elijah. How He went about doing this we do not know. Did He speak audibly to her? Did He appear in a dream or a vision? Did He quietly work on her heart so that when the prophet appeared, without even understanding why, she found herself obeying and believing him? We can only theorize and assume.

Jesus' allusion to this incident in Luke 4:16-27 suggests that there was something about the widow woman – her attitude toward God and her understanding of Him – which made her the beneficiary and recipient of God's divine providence and provision. Rejected and scoffed at by His fellow Nazarenes, Jesus drew their attention to the incident in 1 Kings 17:

> *But I tell you of a truth, many widows were in Israel in the days of Elias, when the heaven was shut up three years and six months,*

*when great famine was throughout the land; But unto none of them
was Elias sent, save unto Serepta, a city of Sidon, unto a woman that
was a widow.*

Jesus was underlining the stark contrast between this widow woman from
Zarephath and the Jews who had gathered in the synagogue that Sabbath
day. Their religious pride and haughtiness made them scoff and sneer at His
proclamation that He was the one sent to preach the gospel to the poor, to
heal the brokenhearted, preach deliverance to the captives, recovery of sight
to the blind, and to liberate those who are bruised. Far from the God they
proclaimed to worship, they were unable see that the prophecy of Isaiah was
being fulfilled right before their very eyes. They missed the greatest good that
could have ever come to them.

According to Jesus, the other widows in Israel at the time of the drought
were also in the same boat.

God did not draw a straw nor did He did cast lots to select the Zarephath
widow. She, in a way which is not explicitly revealed to us, was in touch
with Him so that He was able to command her, knowing she would obey.

God never stands far off from us. But we must draw near to Him and
He will draw near to us. We must draw near to God with a true heart in full
assurance of faith (Hebrews 10:22). We must ever come boldly to God's
throne of grace (Hebrews 4:16).

Asaph concluded, *"It is good for me to draw near to God: I have put
my trust in the Lord God, that I may declare all thy works" (Psalm 73:28).*

Let us draw near.

## WE MUST LET GO

We have to let go of our human reasoning and common sense rationalizations which prompt us to rely on ourselves, our spouses, our finances,
our friends, our relatives, our health, or our possessions – the people, insti-
tutions, and systems which we feel we need to live and survive. Instead we
need to acknowledge and understand that it is in God that we live and move
and have any being.

The widow woman had *"a handful of meal in a barrel, and a little oil in
a cruse" (1 Kings 17:12).* This was the only means of sustenance and survival
for her and her son. She only had enough... and then they would both die. She

was relying on the meal and the oil to keep her and her son alive for a few more days. It was all that she had – all that was tangible, logical, and reasonable. Her reasoning and common sense told her that after this was finished she would die – and her son too! She was not being unreasonable to think that way.

But God told her to give up her only means of sustenance. Let it go. Feed the prophet first. The prophet did not arrive carrying a bag of meal with him, nor a fresh jug filled with oil. He did not in any way make it easier for her to let go, except for his word of promise.

His directive was for her to make a cake for him first from what she had available, and then to make a cake for her and her son, promising that she would find that the barrel of meal would not waste, nor the jug of oil fail until God sent rain again.

But she had already heard from God. So whatever inner struggles she might have had, she let go of them, obeyed the man of God, and gave up her only means of survival for her and her son.

## WE MUST EMBRACE GOD'S PROMISES

The widow woman let go of her former trusts and embraced the promise of the man of God. She did this by obeying. She went and did according to the word spoken by Elijah.

She did not run away, nor hold on to what she had. She did not critically analyze her condition and make a common sense decision. She was at the end of her rope. She and her son were going to die. She did not remonstrate with and vilify the prophet, saying: *"How could you ask me to do something like this? Don't you see I am a widow? I have nothing left. My son and I are going to die. We only have one last meal. How could you be so cruel, selfish, and uncaring?"*

No. She let go – and she embraced the promise of the man of God. *She believed it to be true.*

Embracing is resting, putting our weight on, staying on God and believing Him to be true. It means trusting His words in spite of our circumstances – no matter how dire.

Job's wife found herself unable to do this. It was impossible for her to let go of her common sense rationalizations. To embrace any promise of God was totally out of her league. Her common sense and reasoning told her that any God who could allow this calamity to happen to her family was unkind, unfair, unrighteous, unjust, and cruel.

*"He doesn't deserve my trust and love. I prefer to curse him and die" (Job 2:9).*

The widow believed, let go, embraced, and lived!

In venturing wholly on God, we must let go of the tangible and embrace the truth of the intangible!

## WE MUST GIVE ALL

The widow made a cake for Elijah first – just as he had asked her. In spite of her destitution, she gave all she had.

There was another destitute widow who gave all she had – two mites, but Jesus drew His disciples' attention to her, favorably comparing her with the rich men who cast their great gifts into the treasury. *"Of a truth I say unto you, that this poor widow hath cast in more than they all: For all these have of their abundance cast in unto the offerings of God: but she of her penury hath cast in all the living that she had" (Luke 21:3-4).*

Giving has more to do with our focus, the condition of our hearts – love, humility, and reliance on God, rather than any amount of money we give. In God's economy, it is certainly not "the more you give the more you get." It is all about a heart of love and obedience, and trust.

Those who tell us that if we give fifty, one hundred, or two hundred dollars to their ministry, God will bless us in proportion to the gift have no biblical basis for this. I do not doubt those who say that they gave as directed by some minister of the gospel and God tripled their finances. Who am I to doubt a person's testimony? But where do we see this in the Bible? What is the biblical basis for such teaching?

According to Scripture, it is not how much, or what ministry we give to, but our heart of obedience to God that matters most. God wants us to know Him and trust Him only, to embrace His promises so that we willingly venture wholly on Him and allow no other trusts to intrude.

There is a lesson here for all of us who have sat beside our dried-up brooks, our broken dreams, our messed up relationships, wealth that has taken wings, and broken health. Let us refocus – not on ourselves, but on God. Let Him direct our giving. It isn't always money, it could be our time, ourselves, our skills and abilities, our talents and natural abilities. Let's give to God whatever He requires of us.

The widow put herself and her son last and the need of the prophet first. When we venture wholly on God, we have to do just that. God and His demands no longer take second place. He becomes first. We give all that He demands.

Abraham gave his son – *His only son whom he loved,* just as God demanded. He rose up early in the morning and saddled his donkey. He took two of his young men, Isaac his son, and the wood for the burnt offering. On Moriah, he built an altar, laid the wood in order, bound his son Isaac, and laid him on the altar upon the wood. Then he stretched forth his hand and took the knife to slay his son, just as God demanded.

Does this sound frightening, this giving all? This putting of ourselves and our needs last and the demands of God first?

It would be frightening if God was unjust, unrighteous, unfair, and unreliable, but He isn't. Abraham knew in his heart that this God who gave him his son from his dead loins, had the power to raise him up again from death. He was a God to trust and believe (Hebrews 11:19).

He ventured wholly on this God. He gave all he had – his only son.

When we reflect on the character of God – who He is – we know that we can venture on Him. He is a God who cannot fail, who never goes back on His Word. He is a God who is able to do *"exceeding abundantly above all we ask or think, according to the power that worketh in us" (Ephesians 3:19).* He is a God who is righteous in all His ways.

## GOD IS ALWAYS WORKING BUT WE WILL SEE THE MIRACULOUS WHEN WE VENTURE WHOLLY ON HIM

*Dried-up brooks are frightening, but they can be the setting for the miraculous.* As we venture wholly on God, as we seek His face, as we trust in Him and are obedient to His words, the impossible will happen. The barrel of meal will not fail... until the Lord sends rain upon the earth. There will be more than enough to live on... until the rains fall.

As the woman risks all by making the prophet a cake first, the miraculous happens. God continually supplies flour and oil for this woman, her son, and the prophet until the drought stops.

The impossible will happen. We will experience miraculous provision – which we cannot explain to anyone. In the time of drought we will survive and live always with enough meal in the barrel and oil in the cruse. Enough.

In 1995 and for several years before, I was unable to save any money. At the end of every month, after paying my mortgage and the business places I still owed, I would have practically nothing left. In July 1995, a friend visited us from another island, and after dinner she explained that at their church, because of the economic downturn, many of the members had lost their jobs. She asked me for a donation for the men who had lost their jobs. I was as poor as a church mouse, but I told her I would see how I could help.

After she left, I asked my sister, who was then the Minister of Education, if she had asked her for any help. She had not. I was askance. How could she ask me, a poor teacher, for help and not ask my sister? I told my Dad about it and he agreed that this was quite unreasonable since I had just built a house.

Inexplicably though, when I got paid at the end of the month, I somehow felt like sending a donation for these folks. So before I paid out any bills, I bought twenty US dollars which I sent with a card and a short note.

On September 5th that same year, Hurricane Luis passed close to Montserrat. It did not do as much damage as Hugo, but it blew the shingles off the roof of my house. A local surveyor assessed the damage for the insurance company and gave me a figure. I was satisfied. When the overseas adjudicator arrived and inspected, he decided I should be given more. It was enough to pay off every single debt I had incurred.

From then on, I was left only with my monthly mortgage and insurance payments, which I was able to manage with my salary. For the first time in years, at the end of the month of October or November 1995, I began saving money from my salary.

I am sure that many of you reading this have had similar experiences.
Venturing on God will bring the miraculous as it did for the widow woman.
God never fails His children. He cannot fail.

## THIS GOD NEVER LETS US GO

Even when we flounder, are perplexed, and find it hard to trust in God and venture wholly on Him, He never lets us go. He holds us up in spite of how we may feel.

The widow woman had all but resigned herself to death. Her hope was gone – dried up. *"I'm gathering two sticks... that we may eat it and die" (1 Kings 17:12)*. She had nothing else and nothing more to hold on to. Her brook had dried up. But God was not going to let her go. He had plans for survival, for enough – for more than enough, for abundance of rain. He sent Elijah to the woman for her to sustain him, so that she in turn would experience a great miracle of divine provision and providence.

So even though we may feel let down, we are never let down. God will never let us go. Never. Even at times when we find it difficult – perhaps almost impossible – to venture wholly on God, to hold on to His promises, to stand on His Word, to rely on Him, He is always there, holding His children up. *He never lets go of their hands.*

When we were teenagers, one of my sisters almost drowned at a church beach picnic. She ventured out in rough seas because she was daring and not afraid of anything. But two very large swells came upon her in quick succession, far too much for her swimming ability and prowess. She was close to a dear brother from the church. She held on to him and he held her. The first wave took them both under and then the next one did. For a while they did not surface. It was too much for our mother. I remember her just walking away.

When it was all over and they came to shore she told us, "I thought I was going to drown, but this brother never let go of my hand. As I was under the water, I could feel him holding on to my hand."

That's like God. The woman looked at the diminishing meal and oil and predicted her death and that of her son. She resigned herself to her fate. But God was not about to let her go.

The young man mentioned earlier who lost his job in the UK, related that though several times he had come to the point of wanting to take his life, he was being held up by God, even though it felt as if his prayers had become one-sided conversations. He shares:

"Although coming close to these brinks, there was always something or someone keeping me back from crossing the threshold. I remember a discussion a friend of mine had with me once when we were watching the news in Montserrat. He said, 'suicide is a permanent answer to a temporary situation.'"

*Something or someone.* God was holding him up, holding him fast, never letting go of his hand – even in his deepest, darkest moments, when he really had no strength of his own to go on. God placed various people in his life to offer help and encouragement: friends, family, and brethren from the church who reached out to him, prayed for him, and sent him scripture messages. *God was never letting go of his hand.*

Like others, you may have experienced (and perhaps still experience) times in your life when you felt you had no more strength to hold on. Barred gates. Closed doors. Hope all but gone. Brook all dried up.

But God will never, ever, ever let go of your hand. This God holds us fast, even when our faith would fail. We may think we are falling, but we are not. We may think we won't survive, but we will. We may believe we are going under, but we won't.

> My Captain leads me forth
> To conquest and a crown.
> The feeblest saint shall win the day,
> Though death and hell obstruct the way. [6]

## ONLY GOD SENDS RAIN

That was the point of the three and a half year drought. As Walvoord and Zuck state, "Baal-worshippers believed that their god was the god of rain. The drought brought on by the true God, showed that He, not Baal, controls the weather." [7]

It is not the government, not the economists, and not the programs to that stimulate new economic activity and growth.

It is not the church activities, the hustle and the bustle of church life, our programs, or plans that bring rain to a church that is dry and parched, nonchalant, and self-satisfied.

It's not about our abilities, training, knowledge, talents, and skills. It is about God. The answer is in Him. Jeremiah 14:22 makes this explicit: *"Are there any among the vanities of the Gentiles that can cause rain? Or can the heavens give showers? Art not thou he, O Lord our God? Therefore we will wait upon thee: for thou hast made all these things."*

The Bible explains the sequence of events in James 5:17-18: *"Elijah was a man subject to like passions as we are, and he prayed earnestly that it might not rain: and it rained not on the earth by the space of three years and six months. And he prayed again, and the heaven gave rain, and the earth brought forth her fruit."*

We waste our time and our trust when we look to men, governments, presidents, prime ministers, and leaders. God sends rain. Only God. And when His people humble themselves and pray, seek God's face, and turn from their wicked ways, God hears from Heaven and forgives our sins and heals our land.

God controls the weather and only He can send the rain on our dry and parched land.

## ENOUGH AND MORE THAN ENOUGH

The major question of this study has been: "How is God more than enough when we come to the end of all that we have that we consider indispensable to our survival and sustenance? How is He enough when our brook dries up, when life is unfair, when we are dealt far more than we can humanly bear?

In practical terms, how is God enough or more than enough when He appears not to answer our prayers, and when we feel let down, misled, disappointed, and perhaps even mistreated by Him?

The account in 1 Kings 17, numerous other biblical examples, and the personal testimonies included in this book tell us that God Himself is enough and more than enough.

Asaph found God to be more than enough for all his needs and questions. He was troubled about the unfairness of life, and the fact that the wicked seemed to be more prosperous than the righteous. He was on the verge of throwing in the towel, even feeling that he had served God in vain! His brook of faith and trust were just about dried up.

But he went to the sanctuary where he was reminded about who God is. As he drew near to God, God became his strength and his portion. He was able to conclude, *"Truly God is good to Israel, even to such as are of a clean heart" (Psalm 73:1). "Nevertheless I am continually with thee: thou has holden me by my right hand" (Psalm 73:23). "But it is good for me to draw near to God: I have put my trust in the Lord God, that I may declare all thy works" (Psalm 73:28).*

And Abraham? Blessings came in downpours (Genesis 22:17-18):

*By myself have I sworn, saith the Lord, for because thou hast done this thing, and hast not withheld thy son, thine only son: That in blessing I will bless thee, and in multiplying I will multiply thy seed as the stars of the heaven, and as the sand which is upon the sea shore; and thy seed shall possess the gate of his enemies; And in thy seed shall all the nations of the earth be blessed; because thou has obeyed my voice.*

And Job? Job received far more than the restoration of his possessions and children. He had a mighty, life-changing revelation of God. His spiritual eyes were opened and he saw God for who He was, not what he felt God should be.

*"I have heard of thee by the hearing of the ear; but now mine eye seeth thee" (Job 42:5).*

All his life, Job had tied in his material blessings with his upright living and moral integrity. He somehow felt that there was something in him that merited God's favor, and his riches, health, and prominence were proof of this. That's why he was so baffled by his suffering. What had he done to deserve such suffering?

God's revelation of Himself to Job allowed him to let go of his feelings of merit, entitlement, and focus on God's sovereignty, His power, His justice, His fairness, His goodness, and His strength.

Job came to understand that God is sovereign and does all things well. Job knew nothing in comparison to God .

*"I will lay mine hand upon mine mouth" (Job 40:4).*

He came to understand that we could never deserve, merit, or earn God's favor and love.

*"Wherefore I abhor myself and repent in dust and as he" (Job 42:6).*

He learned that the removal of his earthly joys and ties in no way suggested that God was angry with him or had forsaken him.

His suffering was worth this lesson.

And what of Elijah and the widow?

They had more than enough until the rains came. First Kings 17:16 tells us *"the barrel of meal wasted not, neither did the cruse of oil fail, according to the word of the Lord, which he spake by Elijah."* As she obeyed the prophet and trusted in His word and in the God of Israel, *"she, he and her house did eat many days" (1 Kings17:15).*

Imagine her going from preparing the last meal for her son and herself, and preparing to die, to having more than enough to live on for many days!

The two men whose stories I related in this book are both twenty-first century, true-life examples of children of God – believers who sat beside their brook, saw it lessen to a trickle, and eventually dry up. Not only were their finances drying up, but they felt as if their faith, hope, trust, and confidence in God were also drying up.

The man whose story appears at the beginning of the book has experienced panic, felt fear, and become worried and anxious, yet...

He has never become homeless. His children and family have never had to go without a meal. All his children have been to university. His last child was recently awarded a scholarship to a prominent university in the city where they live.

Every single miraculous day, his empty barrel has had enough meal and his cruse has had enough oil. Every single miraculous day, he has found enough hope in the barrel and enough faith in the cruse to keep going on. He cannot explain it, for many times he felt he had reached the end of his rope, but enough strength, enough courage, enough hope, and enough trust are being provided to him day after miraculous day.

*"The barrel of meal has not wasted nor the cruse of oil failed."*

He still struggles, but every single miraculous day of his life, amidst all the ups and downs, disappointments and doubts, doors that remain shut, gates that continue to be barred, promises that seem only to be mirages in his wilderness, God has been holding him fast, even when he feels as if his faith would fail.

"Every morning," he has said to me, "I find myself with the strength and courage to go on, to pray, to trust, to keep going, even when I don't feel like it."

The other young man told me he is thankful that he didn't throw in the towel. He says there is sunshine now. He has a job – a far cry from the halcyon days of his job as a Telecoms engineer, but to use his own words: "God is good. He has kept me. I thank Him for keeping me and also for winking at my ignorance in my moment of despair."

They, like the widow woman, have enough and more than enough as God daily provides for their needs – grace, mercy and peace, endurance and courage. God's means of supply never runs dry.

As we venture wholly on God, we will find Him to be our all in all the vicissitudes of life – its ups and its downs, its joys and its sorrows, its pleasures and its pain.

We will find in Him our portion and our strength forever as we draw near and run to Him, and as we acknowledge every day, in good times and in bad, in health and in sickness, in wealth and in poverty, that we need Him, and that we can't even walk without Him holding our hands.

He will send the ravens, the prostitutes, the prophets, the widows, the wasted days, and manna in the wilderness to supply our every need.

Relationships will turn into messes, finances will diminish, health will disappear, our strength will fail – every earthly thing can dry up. Every earthly thing is sinking sand, but God is our rock.

We have lost our focus and are ill-advised when we trust in people and in things – spouses, friends, relatives, possessions, career success, health, finances, prominence, position – anything that life offers. These things are not trustworthy. The list of those who take their lives in despair includes the wealthy, the healthy, the wise, famous celebrities. They had all the things we feel are necessary for survival. It is possible to have it all and find that you have nothing at all.

*"It is only in God that we have all things that pertain to life and godliness" (1 Peter 1:3-11).*

If we are to be instructed by this narrative in 1 Kings 17, let us believe and know that God is always there, working on behalf of His people. He is behind the scenes, working all things together for our good and for His glory. He never sleeps and He never slumbers.

It matters not if the dried-up brooks are part of His chastening. God is there, on our side, preparing for our future, providing even in impossible situations, making a way for His people.

God is not asleep. He is not unkind and He is never late! He is always at work on behalf of His children and will work so that our dried-up brooks – be they a result of our sin, wrong decisions, mistakes, or no wrong we have done – will overflow to "His glory and our best good." [8]

God is enough and more than enough because His Word is His bond. He cannot go back on His Word. He watches over His Word to make sure that it is fulfilled, for Heaven and earth may pass away, but His Word cannot and will not fail.

He is enough and more than enough because He listens to and hears our prayers, even our anxious prayers, for the eyes of the Lord are upon the righteous and His ears are open unto their cry (Psalm 34:15).

God is *always* at work on behalf of His people.

The barrel of meal may waste away and the cruse of oil may fail. The ravens may stop coming with their bread and flesh. The brook you have sat by to sustain you may have lessened to a trickle and dried up. But His brooks never dry up.

His brooks of grace, mercy, love, peace, forgiveness, goodness and compassion never go dry. He never forgets any of His children. Things never get out of His control.

When we believe this to be true and run to Him in our troubles, resting in Him, allowing Him to hold us when we cannot hold on any longer, we will find Him to be the God of more than enough – our strength and our portion forever.

God will send the rain. He will *"restore to you the years that the locust hath eaten, the cankerworm, and the caterpillar, and the palmerworm, my great army which I sent among you. And ye shall eat in plenty, and be satisfied, and praise the name of the Lord your God, that hath dealt wondrously with you, and my people shall never be ashamed." (Joel 2:25-26).*

Hope will be fully restored. Joy will spring forth as a new day.

Elijah told the widow woman that there would always be enough meal and oil until the Lord sent the rain on the earth. And did the rains come! The rains fell in torrents. First Kings 18:45 describes the event: *"And it came to pass in the mean while, that the heaven was black with clouds and wind, and there was a great rain."*

The rains will fall. God will send the rains:

- The rains of His presence.
- The rains of His peace.
- The rains of His favor.
- The rains of restored joy and hope in God.

- The rains of supernatural strength and courage to go on, in spite of everything.
- The rains of supernatural faith to continue to believe.
- *The rains of hope no longer deferred!*

God will come and He will shower us with the rains of His presence, His peace, His favor, His grace, and His mercy, restoring our joy, supernatural strength, and courage. He will answer our prayers.

God will awake *"as a dream when one awaketh" (Psalm 73:20)*, and He will send the rain.

When all the things that seem to be against us to drive us to despair and all we have so far relied on for our survival and sustenance dry up, remember:

*"The people that know their God shall be strong and do exploits" (Daniel 11:32).*

So let those who sit at dried-up brooks who feel and have felt like giving up learn to draw near to God. Look to His face, not just His hands. Sit at His feet and learn of Him. Wait on Him. How long did Abraham, Job, Joseph, David, and Elijah wait?

Desire Him more than your very food or any other earthly joy.

Delight yourself in Him and acknowledge Him in all your ways.

Let go of all other trusts – earthly resources, good health, education, training, abilities, talents, jobs, entitlements, family, relationships, spouses, children, friends, and material possessions. These are all sinking sand. They will dry up. They will fade away. Don't put your trust in them.

Embrace God's promises and see Him as the only solid rock on which to stand.

He will make your feet like hinds' feet. You will find yourself walking in the most difficult and impossible of places for He will be your joy and your portion forever.

Asaph was really quite misguided in his assumptions about the prosperous wicked. All people in this life have troubles of one kind or another. The wealthy – be they godly or ungodly – have troubles like other men and are often plagued more than others. God is our only sure foundation and God's purpose for His children is always for our own good.

*"He who holds us in His hands – has no problems, only plans...* [9]

We can have an abundant entrance into the everlasting Kingdom of God in spite of dried-up brooks. We will then be able to sing as Habakkuk did:

*Although the fruit tree shall not blossom, neither shall fruit be in the vines; the labour of the olive shall fail, and the fields shall yield no meat; the flock shall be cut off from the fold, and there shall be no herd in the stalls: Yet I will rejoice in the Lord, I will joy in the God of my salvation. The Lord God is my strength, and he will make my feet like hinds feet, and he will make me to walk upon mine high places (Habakkuk 3:17-19).*

Furthermore, *"the sufferings of this present time are not worthy to be compared with the glory which shall be revealed in us" (Romans 8:18).*

After all, our story does not end here.

# Chapter 6

## Final Word

"*For the Lord thy God bringeth thee into a good land,
a land of brooks and water...*"
*Deuteronomy 8:7*

To You – at the Dried-up Brook

Dear Child of God,

Believe God.
Trust God.

"Trust in Him with all thine heart; and lean not unto thine own understanding" (Proverbs 3:5).

"In all thy ways acknowledge him, and he shall direct thy path" (Proverbs 3:6).

"Rest in the Lord, and wait patiently for Him" (Psalm 37:7).

"The Lord redeemeth the soul of his servants: and none of them that trust in Him shall be desolate" (Psalm 34:22).

"The eyes of the Lord are upon the righteous and His ears are open unto their cry" (Psalm 34:15).

"Instead of the thorn shall come up the fir tree and instead of the brier shall come up the myrtle tree and it shall be to the Lord for a name, for an everlasting sign that shall not be cut off" (Isaiah 55:13).

"And I will restore to you the years that the locust hath eaten, the cankerworm, and the caterpillar, and the palmerworm, my great army which I sent among you. And ye shall eat in plenty, and be satisfied, and praise the name of the Lord your God that hath dealt wondrously with you: and my people shall never be ashamed" (Joel 2:25-26).

"For thou, Lord, wilt bless the righteous; with favour wilt thou compass him as with a shield" (Psalm 5:12).

"But though our outward man perish, yet the inward man is renewed day by day. For our light affliction which is but for a moment, worketh for us a far more exceeding and eternal weight of glory; While we look not at the things which are seen, but the things which are not seen: for the things which are seen are temporal, but the things which area not seen are eternal" (2 Corinthians 4:16-18).

# Footnotes

## Chapter 2

[1] UNICEF, "Ethiopia: The Hardest Hit," Drought Disasters, http://www.unicer.org/drought/main.htm, (May 19, 2000).

[2] R. Robinson, "Come Thou Fount of Every Blessing," Public Domain.

## Chapter 3

[1] Dr Archibald D. Hart, *The Hidden Link Between Adrenalin & Stress* (USA: Word Books, 1986), 137.

[2] Gordon Macdonald, *Ordering My Private World* (USA: Oliver Nelson, 1984), 179.

[3] Wayne A. Meeks et al, eds. *The Harper Collins Study Bible* (New York: Harper Collins Publishers, 1989), 548.

## Chapter 4

[1] C.S. Lewis, *A Grief Observed* (England: Faber & Faber, 1966), 5.

[2] H. Robinson, "All In The Name of Jesus," Public Domain.

[3] J. Newton, "Come My Soul Thy Suit Prepare," Public Domain.

[4] Colbert and Joyce Croft, "Can't Even Walk," Public Domain.

[5] G. Rawson, "O Worship the King," Public Domain.

[6] Elie Wiesel, *Night*, (New York: Hill and Wang, 2006), 69.

## Chapter 5

[1] Harold S. Kushner, *When Bad Things Happen to Good People* (USA: Anchor Books, 2004), 10.

[2] Elie Wiesel, *Night*, 76-77.

[3] Bryan Jeffery Leech, "He Who Holds Us in His Hands," © Fred Bock Music Company, 1988. Used by permission of the publisher.

[4] John F. Walvoord and Roy B. Zuck, *The Bible Knowledge Commentary* (USA: David C. Cook, 1983), 524.

[5] Joseph Hart, "Come Ye Sinners, Poor and Needy," Public Domain.

[6] Isaac Watts, "Join All the Glorious Names," Public Domain.

*Footnotes*

7 Walvoord and Zuck, *The Bible Commentary,* 524.

8 Leech, "He Who Holds Us in His Hands."

9 Leech, "He Who Holds Us in His Hands."

www.ingramcontent.com/pod-product-compliance
Lightning Source LLC
Chambersburg PA
CBHW032012040426
42448CB00006B/596